Contents

Executive Summary

In preparing this Country Development Cooperation Strategy (CDCS), the Mission held more than 40 meetings with stakeholders from the Government of the Dominican Republic (GODR), civil society, implementing partners, the private sector, bilateral and multilateral donors, Dominican private sector foundations, church leaders, and United States Government (USG) partners. [1] The Mission made a special effort to talk directly with beneficiaries. We met with beneficiaries in hospitals, HIV/AIDS treatment centers, bateyes (poor, rural communities inhabited primarily by Haitian sugar cane plantation workers), with community leaders and youth in urban slums, and with clients of community justice houses. The Mission proactively reached out to vulnerable groups, in particular people with disabilities, the Lesbian, Gay, Bisexual and Transgender (LGBT) community, women, and youth at risk, so we could hear from them, first hand, their needs and priorities.

Problem Statement

Throughout the consultation process that guided the development of this strategy, citizen security was identified by the Dominicans as a significant challenge to economic growth and development. Citizen security has myriad characterizations, but this strategy applies the definition promulgated at the 2012 Summit of the Americas of 'a democratic civic order that removes the threats posed by violence in the population and enables secure and peaceful coexistence. It concerns, in essence, the effective safeguarding of a broad range of human rights ... including, among others, the right to personal safety, freedom of movement, and the enjoyment of heritage ....'

In addition to advancing social freedoms and well-being, increasing citizen security by reducing crime has a positive effect on investment and therefore sustains and promotes economic growth. A 2005 United Nations Development Program (UNDP) study found that 63 percent of firms in the Dominican Republic cited crime as a major obstacle to investment. A 2007 UNDP study concluded that crime leads to reduced economic growth. The study noted that crime and the perception of crime can contribute to public sector funds being diverted from productive investments to crime prevention measures and divert private funds from investment in business expansion to security improvements to protect existing investments (security guards, alarm systems). The study concluded that economic growth would have increased in the Dominican Republic by 1.8 percent if the GODR had been able to bring its homicide rate down to the level of Costa Rica. Therefore, increasing citizen security by reducing crime can also contribute to promoting economic growth.

---

[1] GODR on at least two occasions, persons with disabilities, LGBT, GBV organizations, private sector, implementing partners.

Goal: The Dominican Republic Improves Citizen Security to Promote Economic Growth

Based on extensive consultations with Dominican colleagues, other donors, and implementing partners, USAID/Dominican Republic adopted as its overarching goal to work with Dominicans to improve citizen security in order to promote economic growth. To help the Dominicans achieve this goal, USAID/Dominican Republic identified three sectors where it will work. Each of these sectors has a corresponding Development Objective that is described below.

Development Objective (DO) 1: Crime Prevention Strengthened

USAID/Dominican Republic will pursue a tripartite approach to crime prevention. It will 1) work with at-risk youth in the country's poorest, most violent, and most densely populated urban areas; 2) improve the basic reading skills of students in targeted poor neighborhoods; and 3) implement systemic reforms to the criminal justice system. Our objective will be to decrease the vulnerability of at-risk youth by keeping them in or reinserting them into school, as well as helping them to find gainful employment through vocational education in sectors projected to grow in the Dominican economy. To keep children in school, USAID/Dominican Republic will focus on strengthening schools in the targeted neighborhoods and encouraging the GODR to expand the USAID-piloted Effective Schools Program (ESP) nationwide. The ESP program has generated learning gains among participants that are significantly greater than those of non-participants, and garnered support from the private sector as well as the GODR. Complementing the improved reading program in primary schools, USAID/Dominican Republic will also support remedial and supplemental reading programs in targeted neighborhoods. At the systemic level, the GODR will be assisted to implement key police reforms and strengthen key justice institutions. The combination of systemic improvements in the justice system, which lead to increased responsiveness of the justice sector to citizen needs, and a drop in crime in the most crime-ridden neighborhoods in the country, should help to create an improved sense of citizen security.

Development Objective 2: Increased Resilience of People to the Impact of Climate Change

USAID/Dominican Republic will work to increase the resilience of people to the impacts of climate change, thereby reducing physical insecurity and economic losses caused by the havoc of climate change-induced severe weather events and sea level rise. Specifically, USAID/Dominican Republic will develop and improve municipal land use planning to integrate climate change information and increase the adoption of adaptation measures at the local level, with a particular focus on water source protection and disaster risk reduction in Santo Domingo and Santiago, the two most populous cities in the country. These urban areas are home to the majority of the country's population and reflect the Mission's concentration on reducing the vulnerability of these marginalized populations. The program will also work in two or three targeted coastal towns, where the tourism industry is already at risk because of climate change impacts, and in selected rural areas that have already suffered the impacts of disasters and global climate change.

Development Objective 3: AIDS-Free Generation Advanced

USAID/Dominican Republic will implement programs to help prevent the spread of HIV/AIDS, improve care for persons with HIV/AIDS, end stigma and discrimination against HIV/AIDS victims and the LGBT community, and reduce gender-based violence (GBV). These efforts will help increase personal security for these vulnerable groups.

Geographic Focus

Crime prevention and Global Climate Change programs (DOs 1 and 2) will focus primarily on the corridor that runs from Santo Domingo north to Puerto Plata. It includes six of the nation's 32 provinces, 70 percent of the Dominican population, and 63 percent of the country's youth. The cities where crime is the highest in the Dominican Republic all also lie within this corridor.[2] For HIV/AIDS, the location of key populations guide where HIV/AIDS investments and services need to be offered, and therefore, DO 3 will not be geographically focused.

Cross-Sectoral Themes: Transparency and Inclusion of Marginalized Populations

Throughout the implementation of this CDCS, there are two cross cutting issues that affect all sectors: 1) transparency and accountability and 2) addressing the needs of marginalized populations. USAID/Dominican Republic will support a limited number of key systemic reforms to promote transparency across ministries and has identified within each of the Development Objectives potential areas where USAID/Dominican Republic's investments can contribute to greater transparency. To address the needs and protect the rights of marginalized populations, including women, people without official identification documents, the LGBT community and people with disabilities, USAID/Dominican Republic will also identify opportunities to protect and promote their rights with systemic and sector-specific approaches.

Results

Working in concert with like-minded stakeholders, by 2018, USAID/Dominican Republic investments will:

- Help more than 80,000 youth aged 11-24 to finish school, receive vocational training, find jobs, and develop better life skills;
- Help more than 60,000 people through crime prevention at the community level;
- Improve reading skills of 100,000 students in 400 public primary schools;
- Enable four municipalities (including the major cities of Santo Domingo and Santiago) to incorporate climate change information into their land use planning, reducing vulnerability to natural disasters;
- Reach 60,000 at-risk youth through programs in HIV prevention and sexual and reproductive health;

---

[2] Locations with the highest rates of crime are noted here. For robberies: National District, Puerto Plata, Santiago, San Cristobal and Santo Domingo. For assaults: National District, La Romana, San Cristobal, Santiago, and Santo Domingo. Kidnappings: National District, San Cristobal, Santiago, Santo Domingo, and La Vega. Rape: Barahona, Peravia, and Santo Domingo.

- Reduce the HIV Mother to Child transmission rate to below two percent; and
- Reduce the HIV prevalence rate in key populations to below three percent.

Policy Dialogue

USAID/Dominican Republic would be significantly underestimating the impact it can have if it did not factor in what can be accomplished, without any investment of money, through a systematic approach to policy dialogue. During the next five years, outside of the sectoral confines of the DOs, USAID/Dominican Republic will initiate dialogue to ensure that investments USAID, and others, have made are sustainable and fully adopted by the GODR. A few of the results expected from USAID/Dominican Republic's systemic policy dialogue include:

- Ministry of Education (MOE) adopts the USAID funded Effective Schools Program teaching methodology for reading and math nationwide;
- Ministry of Health expands the USAID funded Centers of Excellence for Maternal and Child health program nationwide;
- Performance-based budget planning methodology expanded from Health, Education, Labor and Finance Ministries to other Ministries;
- The Ministry of Education makes new classrooms accessible to students with special needs and develops a curriculum and teacher training that encourages special needs students to attend school;
- The Ministry of Health's planned renovation of 36 hospitals incorporates universal designs for accessibility; and
- The Ministry of Health assumes increasing financial responsibility for funding HIV services.

USAID/Dominican Republic's ability to initiate policy dialogue simultaneously on so many fronts is a testament to the cumulative efforts, and consequent influence, of all the USAID/Dominican Republic staff who have worked over the last 50 years for the benefit of the Dominican people. During the course of this strategy, USAID/Dominican Republic's relationship with the GODR will continue to evolve as a relationship of partners, dedicated to the mutual security and economic prosperity of both nations.

Development Context

Country Overview and Development Challenges

The Dominican Republic is the Caribbean region's largest economy with a gross domestic product (GDP) in 2012 estimated to be $98.74 billion (three times the size of Guatemala's). The Dominican economy, which had experienced impressive growth over many years, has slowed since 2011, from a growth rate of 4.5 percent in 2011 to 3.9 percent in 2012 and a projected 3 percent growth rate in 2013[3].The Dominican Republic's projected growth rate (3.8 percent) for 2013 is higher than the Caribbean average of 3.5 percent, and the projected growth rate of Haiti (6 percent), Nicaragua, Chile, and Bolivia (5 percent), Ecuador (3.5 percent), Honduras (3.3 percent) and Guatemala (3.2 percent)[4].

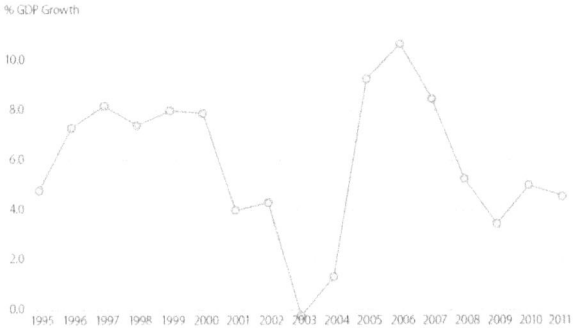

Source: Economist Intelligence Unit

Inequality

The Dominican Republic is classified as an upper middle income country. However, the country's economic progress masks high levels of inequality that permeate Dominican society. Forty percent of the population receives less than 10 percent of the country's wealth, while the wealthiest 10 percent account for more than 40 percent of the country's income.[5] More than 40 percent of the Dominican people live in poverty. The Gini coefficient, which measures a country's income equality (on a scale of 0-100, with higher being more unequal), for the Dominican Republic is 47.2[6] in 2012, better than it was in 2000 at 52, but worse in comparison to other countries in Latin America: El Salvador 46.9; Peru 46.0; Argentina 45.8; Nicaragua 40.5[7].

A nation's prosperity also correlates with the level of parity between women and men, and there continues to be considerable gender inequality in the Dominican Republic. In 2012, the Dominican Republic received an overall ranking of 89 out of 135 countries in the World Economic Forum's (WEF)

---

[3] Central Intelligence Agency (CIA) World Factbook 2012. www.cia.gov/library/publications/the-world-factbook/geos/dr.html

[4] Economic Commission for Latin American and the Caribbean (ECLAC), Updated Economic Overview of Latin American and the Caribbean, 2012.

[5] Economic Commission for Latin America and the Caribbean. Social Panorama of Latin America, 2012, news article November 28, 2012.

[6] CIA World Factbook 2012

[7] Ibid.

Gender Gap Index.[8] The Dominican Republic's ranking has steadily declined since 2009, when it ranked 67 out of 134 countries. According to the Inter-American Development Bank (IDB), there is also a gender salary gap of 16 percent, indicating that women receive lower salaries for the same work.

Unemployment

A gender gap also exists in terms of unemployment. From 2003 to 2011, the average unemployment rate among men was 9.9 percent, while for women it was 25.3 percent.[9] In 2011, 14.6 percent of the country's 4.5 million workers, or 668,000 people, were unemployed.[10] In 2012, the national unemployment rate dropped slightly to 13 percent, but youth unemployment exceeded 30 percent.

Crime and Violence

The fear of crime is palpable in the Dominican Republic. In 2012, 65 percent of the population reported feeling less secure than they did five years ago.[11] Crime statistics validate that the fear is justified. Homicide rates in the Dominican Republic have almost doubled from 2002 to 2012, from 14 to 24 per 100,000 people, making it the fourth most violent country in the Caribbean. According to the 2012 Latin American Public Opinion Project (LAPOP) survey, 25 percent of Dominican Republic citizens report having been robbed or assaulted in the last year.[12]

Gangs and drugs are also major concerns. In the 2012 LAPOP survey, the Dominican Republic is ranked first of all countries in Latin America and the Caribbean in terms of people reporting that their neighborhoods were affected by gangs (48.6 percent in the Dominican Republic vs. 29.6 percent in Honduras). While the characteristics, power, and actions of gangs vary dramatically throughout the region, this nevertheless represents a troublesome perception for Dominicans. In 2012, 27.9 percent of the Dominican population reported seeing the sale of drugs in their neighborhood, up from 18.4 percent in 2008. According to the Dominican Attorney General's Office, during the period 2005 to May 2012, 40.6 percent of crimes were drug related. In 2009, more than 24,000 drug-related arrests were made in the Dominican Republic, of which 70 percent (17,000 people) were young offenders.

Drug trafficking is also on the rise. According to the National Office of Drug Control, drug seizures have more than tripled between 2008 and 2012, and for 2013, in just three weeks, seizures were already at 25 percent of 2012 levels. While this may indicate improved interdiction, it may also be the result of greater drug trafficking along routes through the Caribbean and the increased presence of transnational criminal organizations from Mexico and Central and South America operating in Dominican territory.

Violence against Women

Although there are no national statistics on GBV, Dominicans have expressed their perception and voiced their concern that the incidence of GBV is extensive and on the rise. In December 2012, the

---

[8] World Economic Forum, 2012 Gender Gap Report. http://www3.weforum.org/docs/WEF_GenderGap_Report_2012.pdf
[9] Dominican National Office of Statistics (Oficina Nacional de Estadisticas)
[10] Dominican Central Bank
[11] AmericasBarometer 2012
[12] DR1 Daily News report, June 21, 2011. www.dr1.com

Attorney General stated that the number of GBV complaints filed in Santo Domingo in 2012 had nearly doubled over 2011, and that 85 percent of these cases had been filed by women aged 18-35. According to the 2007 Demographic Health Survey (DHS), 9.7 percent of women aged 15 - 49 experienced physical violence and 10.1 percent experienced sexual violence in 2007.[13] In addition, 29.8 percent of women ages 15 - 49 reported at some point in their lives being victims of domestic abuse. Of those who had experienced sexual violence, 38.5 percent experienced their first aggression before the age of 20, with 6.5 percent of respondents stating they were younger than 10 years old when they first experienced sexual violence.[14]

The Dominican Republic is also identified as a source, transit and destination country for sex trafficking and forced labor by the U.S. Department of State's 2012 Trafficking in Persons Report. Dominican trafficking is widespread, and victims have been found in or repatriated from 18 countries around the world, primarily in the Americas and Europe. Between 2007 and 2010, Dominican victims accounted for about 1 percent of the victims detected in Western and Central Europe and about 3 percent of the victims detected in the Americas.[15]

Exclusion and Discrimination

In the Dominican Republic, the poor, people with disabilities, persons infected with or affected by HIV, undocumented Dominicans and Haitians, women, and members of the lesbian, gay, bisexual, and transgender community suffer from discrimination and exclusion from Dominican society.

Estimates of the number of Haitians living in the Dominican Republic vary widely, from as low as 450,000 to a high of 1.2 million[16]. Undocumented Haitians living in the Dominican Republic have complained of living in fear of being deported, abused by authorities, exploited by employers and unable to register and start their own businesses. Undocumented children, including those of Haitian descent can attend primary school, but cannot attend secondary school. There is growing recognition that Haitians, or Dominicans of Haitian descent, are discriminated against and have unequal access to many social services. The 2012 LAPOP survey reported that 60.6 percent of Dominicans believe that immigrants should be able to access Dominican public services.

Another excluded group is people with disabilities. There is a sizable Dominican population with some kind of disability. The 2010 Dominican Census indicated that 12.3 percent of the population, or 1.1 million people, have some kind of disability. Most people with disabilities are not working and their access to education has been severely limited because most buildings and schools are not physically accessible. A United Nations Educational, Scientific, and Cultural Organization (UNESCO) study, published in December 2012, reported that 70 percent of children with a disability were currently not in school.

[13] Demographic Health Survey 2007. http://www.measuredhs.com/what-we-do/survey/survey-display-291.cfm
[14] Ibid.
[15] "Global Report on Trafficking in Persons 2012." United Nations Office of Drugs and Crime, Dec. 2012. Web. 24 June 2013. <http://www.unodc.org/documents/data-and-analysis/glotip/Trafficking_in_Persons_2012_web.pdf>
[16] European Union, UNFPA, Officina Nacional de Estadistica, Primera Encuesta Nacional de Inmigrantes en la Republic Dominicana ENI-2012, 2012

These vulnerable groups, which amount to a sizable percentage of the Dominican population, live on the margins of Dominican society. Taking into consideration the population disenfranchised because they have a disability, the population excluded because they are undocumented, the young people unemployed, Dominicans who live below the poverty line, the LGBT community, and people affected by and infected with HIV/AIDS, a sizable portion of the Dominican population are directly affected by citizen security issues that extend well beyond just the issue of being a crime victim. Excluding these groups from the benefits generally enjoyed by other Dominicans can pose its own unique citizen security and stability issues.

Poor Business Environment

Today, the Dominican Republic stands at 137 out of 185 economies on the ease of starting a business.[17] The Dominican Republic's economic freedom score was 60.2 in 2012, making its economy the 89th freest of 161 countries analyzed and, within the South and Central America and Caribbean region, the Dominican Republic is ranked 18th out of 29 countries. The chart below, from the 2013 Democracy, Human Rights, and Governance Assessment for the Dominican Republic, shows various obstacles to investment cited by the private sector. Common obstacles cited in both studies are corruption and crime.

CHART 4.1.8-2, OBSTACLES TO INVESTMENT AND DOING BUSINESS IN THE DOMINICAN REPUBLIC

WORLD BANK INVESTMENT CLIMATE SURVEY, 2005	GLOBAL COMPETITIVENESS REPORT, 2012-2013
Electricity	Corruption
Corruption	Inefficient government bureaucracy
Crime	Access to financing
Macroeconomic Instability	Taxes
Uncertain policies and regulations	Inadequately educated workforce
Anticompetitive informal policies	Crime
Access to and cost of financing	Restrictive labor regulations

Sources: World Bank, World Economic Forum.
Note: Issues in both surveys are listed in the order of their stated importance.

Corruption

In the 2012 LAPOP survey, 78 percent of Dominicans indicated that corruption was a problem. The World Economic Forum ranked the Dominican Republic the worst in the world in terms of wasteful government spending (144th of 144 countries) and 142nd in terms of diversion of public funds.[18]

---

[17] World Bank. Doing Business 2013 Country Profile for Dominican Republic.
[18] World Economic Forum's Global Competitiveness Report 2012-2013

Unreliable Electricity

The Dominican Republic has the highest priced energy in the region. The inefficient supply of electricity and ineffective governance of the sector suppresses overall economic growth in the Dominican Republic[19].

Negative Impacts of Climate Change

The Dominican Republic is one of the ten most vulnerable countries in the world to climate change.[20] It is also prone to a variety of natural disasters including hurricanes, earthquakes, floods, and landslides, which can severely impact such a small economy. Sea level rise, warmer weather, and more frequent flooding are global climate change symptoms that are already affecting the Dominican Republic and will continue to negatively impact Dominican development prospects. One study predicted that due to sea level rise, by 2030, the Dominican Republic could lose 29 percent of the Bavaro beach in Punta Cana, one of the country's most profitable tourist destinations[21].

Health and HIV

Maternal and child health, teenage pregnancies, tuberculosis (TB), and HIV, especially among the most-at-risk populations, including women with low levels of education, are all critical public health priorities. In 2012, there were an estimated 44,000 persons with HIV in the Dominican Republic.[22] The HIV epidemic disproportionately affects specific populations, including female sex workers, Men that Have Sex with Men (MSM), Drug Users (DU), and residents of *bateyes*.

Poor Quality of Education

The provision of a quality public education is one of the Dominican Republic's most fundamental challenges. The Dominican Republic ranks 143rd in quality of primary education and 137th in quality of the educational system overall, out of 144 countries worldwide.[23]

U.S. Foreign Policy Alignment

The Dominican Republic is important to advancement of U.S. foreign policy interests for a variety of reasons. The Dominican Republic is a significant U.S. trading partner. There is a sizable Dominican constituency in the United States.[24] The Dominican Republic is also a transit point for illegal drugs, migrant smuggling and human trafficking to the United States, which poses a danger to the stability, well-being and security of Dominican and U.S. citizens.

---

[19] USAID Inclusive Growth Diagnostic: Dominican Republic, 2012
[20] German Watch's Global Climate Risk Index 2013.
[21] The CARIBSAVE Climate Change Risk Atlas: Climate Change Risk Profile for The Dominican Republic, 2012
[22] UNAIDS World Epidemic Update2012
[23] World Economic Forum 2012-2013 report
[24] In 2010, 1,414,703 Dominicans lived in the United States. A little more than half are women (53%).

USAID/Dominican Republic's strategy is consistent with the U.S Government's key global and regional development policies: the National Security Strategy, the Presidential Policy Directive on Global Development, the Quadrennial Diplomacy and Development Review, and the U.S. Government's Strategy for Meeting the Millennium Development Goals. This strategy also aligns with USG regional strategic priorities,[25] including Promoting Social & Economic Opportunity, Clean Energy and Mitigated Effects of Climate Change, Safety of the Hemisphere's Citizens, and Strengthening Effective Institutions of Democratic Governance.

Further, the strategy also aligns with USAID's policies on Gender Equality and Female Empowerment, Disability, and Youth. These USG and USAID strategies and policies are brought together under the USAID Policy Framework for 2011-2015, which guides USAID programming throughout the world. The Development Objectives described in this strategy for the Dominican Republic support the following core development objectives outlined in the Policy Framework:
- Promote Sustainable, Broad-Based Economic Growth.
- Expand and Sustain the Ranks of Stable, Prosperous, and Democratic States.
- Build Resilience and Reduce Climate Change Impacts.
- Promote Global Health and Strong Health Systems.

Under the Caribbean Basin Security Initiative (CBSI), USAID/Dominican Republic provides critical assistance to support two of the three core CBSI objectives: to increase public safety and security through programs to reduce crime and violence, and to strengthen social justice through programs designed to promote justice sector reform, combat government corruption, and assist vulnerable populations at risk of recruitment into criminal organizations. Programming under the initiative will also support USAID's Strategy on Democracy, Human Rights, and Governance.

Under the Global Climate Change Initiative, USAID/Dominican Republic will help advance U.S. global climate change policy, USAID's Climate Change and Development Strategy, and the Obama Administration's global development policy by helping host country partners assess and address climate change in ways that promote country ownership, as well as strengthen governance and inclusive planning processes for climate resiliency. Global Climate Change activities that relate to protection and use of water resources also further the objectives of the USAID Water Strategy and align with USAID's Policy and Program Guidance on Building Resilience to Recurrent Crisis.

This strategy also advances the Obama Administration's High Priority Performance Goal for Global Health, which is to reduce mortality of mothers and children under five, to avert millions of unintended pregnancies, to prevent millions of new HIV infections, and to eliminate some tropical diseases by 2015. USAID/Dominican Republic's programming will help reach the overall global goal of supporting the prevention of more than 12 million new HIV infections, providing direct support to more than four million people on treatment, and supporting care for more than 12 million people through the President's Emergency Plan for AIDS Relief (PEPFAR). USAID/Dominican Republic's HIV programming also supports the Millennium Development Goal 6 to "have halted by 2015 and begun to reverse the spread of HIV/AIDS."

---

[25] As described on the Department of State website: http://www.state.gov/p/wha/rt/index.htm

USAID/Dominican Republic's strategy also supports Goal One of USAID's 2011-2015 Education Strategy: Improved reading skills for 100 million children in primary grades by 2015, and Millennium Development Goal 2 to provide universal access to primary education for all children by 2015.

Alignment with Host Country Development Priorities

In 2010, the GODR adopted its first National Development Strategy (END 2010-2030, in Spanish), a 20-year roadmap of the country's development priorities. It underscored the following high-level development objectives:

1. A democratic state with transparent, ethical institutions, that is socially responsible and participative, guarantees security, and promotes equality and governance;
2. A society with equal rights and opportunities; education, health and quality public service delivery guaranteed to the population; and promotion of decreased poverty and inequality;
3. An economy that is developed territorially and by sector, that is innovative, diversified, and environmentally sustainable; and that generates high, sustained growth, with equality and decent employment; increased global competitiveness;
4. A sustainable society that protects the environment and natural resources, and promotes climate change adaptation.

In the process of developing this CDCS, USAID/Dominican Republic organized several meetings with GODR ministries and their technical staff. In total, USAID/Dominican Republic held over 40 meetings with stakeholders in the GODR, civil society, implementing partners, the private sector, bilateral and multilateral donors, Dominican private sector foundations, churches, and USG partners. USAID/Dominican Republic made a special effort to talk directly with beneficiaries, meeting with them in hospitals, HIV/AIDS treatment centers, bateyes (poor, rural, primarily Haitian sugar cane communities), with community leaders and youth in urban slums; and with clients of community justice houses. USAID/Dominican Republic proactively reached out to vulnerable groups, in particular, people with disabilities, the LGBT community, women, and youth at risk, to hear from them firsthand, what were their development priorities.

Development Hypothesis

Goal: The Dominican Republic Improves Citizen Security to Promote Economic Growth

Indicator:

- Citizen perception of insecurity

To increase citizen security, thereby promoting economic growth, the population of the Dominican Republic must not be threatened by crime and violence, communities must be able to prevent and respond to impacts of climate change, and the population must be healthy and free from stigma, discrimination, and exclusion. The development hypothesis is that by strengthening crime prevention, increasing the resilience of people to the impact of climate change, and reducing the impact of HIV, the Dominican Republic will have more secure and prosperous citizens, leading to greater citizen security and economic growth. Because this approach straddles many aspects of Dominican society, an effective response to improve Dominican citizen security and promote economic growth necessarily requires a multi-sectoral approach.

Sector Focus

Considering the plethora of development challenges, host country priorities, USG initiatives, available funding, an analysis of trade-offs, and USAID/Dominican Republic's comparative advantage, USAID/Dominican Republic identified three Development Objectives for the FY 2014-2018 strategy: Crime Prevention, Global Climate Change (GCC), and HIV/AIDS. The strategy focuses on improving citizen security in order to ensure that rising crime, violence, and corruption do not converge to undo more than 50 years of economic growth and development in the Dominican Republic.

Geographic Focus

Crime prevention and GCC (DOs 1 and 2) will be geographically focused in the corridor which goes from Santo Domingo north to Puerto Plata. It includes six of the nation's 32 provinces, 70 percent of the Dominican population, and 63 percent of youth. The cities where crime is the highest in the Dominican Republic are all located within this corridor.[26] Targeting the most populated regions within this corridor will concentrate efforts and maximize impact. Within this corridor, USAID/Dominican Republic will further refine its target to ensure its programming reaches the most at-risk youth in specific communities. By analyzing data such as level of drug use, neighborhood crime statistics, drug trafficking, number of youth arrested, number of youth participating in gangs, the rate of teenage pregnancy and school dropout rates, programmatic focus within this corridor will be further refined.

Moreover, the Mission will work to coordinate programming across sectors through multiple, complementary interventions. For example, USAID/Dominican Republic crime prevention efforts may target work in a community with high levels of poverty and violence to improve job opportunities for at-risk youth and improve access to justice for the poor, while the HIV program provides health and reproductive counseling to at-risk youth, and the GCC program would help prevent flooding and thus improve physical security for poor families living in that same community.

---

[26] Locations with the highest rates of crime are noted here. For robberies: National District, Puerto Plata, Santiago, San Cristobal and Santo Domingo. For assaults: National District, La Romana, San Cristobal, Santiago, and Santo Domingo. Kidnappings: National District, San Cristobal, Santiago, Santo Domingo, and La Vega. Rape: Barahona, Peravia, and Santo Domingo.

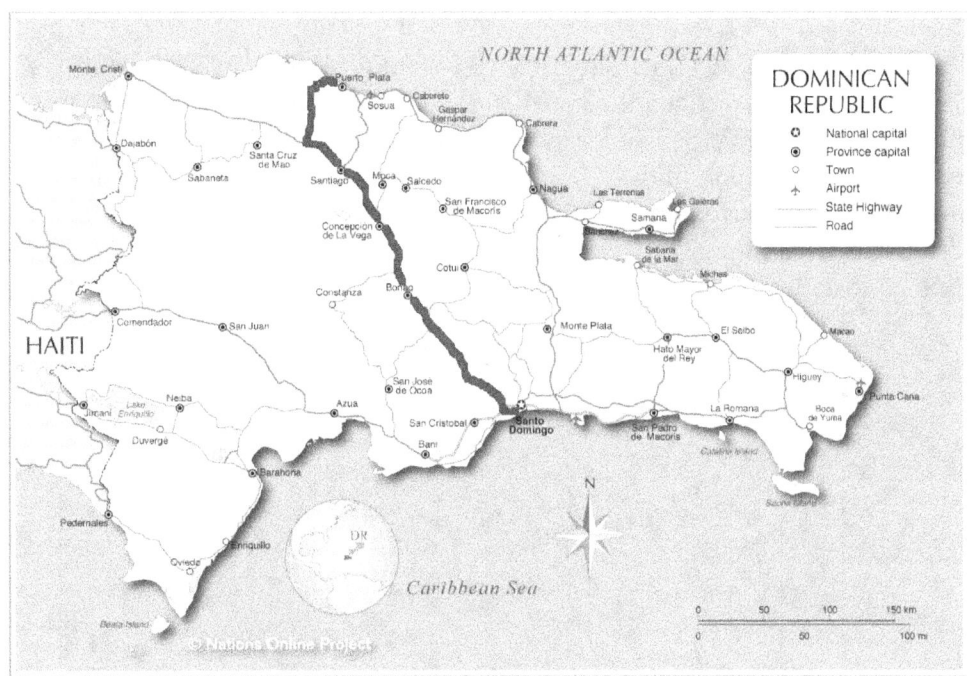

Bold line traces corridor

While most DO1 and 2 resources will be concentrated in this geographic area, it will not be exclusive. In certain cases, such as working in coastal cities on global climate change, some activities will be funded outside of this geographic area. For HIV/AIDS (DO3) the location of key populations will guide where HIV/AIDS investments and services are offered. As mentioned above, some of these key populations (at-risk youth and drug users) may be concentrated in this same urban corridor, but other key populations (people crossing the border and sex workers in tourist areas) are not. Therefore, while DO3 will have significant overlap with DOs 1 and 2 along the Santo Domingo-Puerto Plata corridor, DO3 will not be geographically concentrated.

Cross-Cutting Themes

There are two cross cutting themes that emerged during the course of designing this strategy: transparency and accountability and addressing the needs of marginalized populations. These two themes are incorporated into each of the DOs. However, there are some critical aspects of addressing these issues that require an investment of a limited amount of program resources beyond the DOs in order to ensure that our DO level investments are on target, and to fully capitalize on cross sectoral investments that USAID/Dominican Republic has already made. Some specific areas where USAID/Dominican Republic proposes to make investments in these two cross cutting themes are outlined below.

To address the needs of marginalized populations, reliable data is needed. At the time USAID was preparing for this strategy, there were no nationwide statistics for GBV or people with disabilities. Consequently, USAID/Dominican Republic proposes to conduct, in conjunction with other donors, NGOs, and GODR stakeholders, nationwide GBV and people with disability surveys. With the data generated by these surveys, we will then be able to appropriately target programming for both these groups.

In the area of transparency and accountability, USAID/Dominican Republic has partnered with the GODR to spearhead efforts to overhaul the GODR procurement and budget processes. These efforts work across ministries and have broad and systemic impacts on improving transparency, accountability and efficiency and reducing opportunities for corruption. Because these efforts transcend the three DOs of this strategy, tremendous momentum would be lost if USAID/Dominican Republic transparency programs were limited to HIV, GCC, and crime prevention. Therefore, limited resources will be programmed to capitalize on these on-going transparency efforts.

Indicator:
- Percentage of population that reports being a victim of assault or robbery in the past year

USAID/Dominican Republic will pursue a tripartite approach to crime prevention in the Dominican Republic. It will 1) work with at-risk youth in the country's poorest, most violent, and most densely populated urban areas; 2) improve the basic reading skills of students in targeted poor neighborhoods; and 3) implement systemic reforms to the criminal justice system. The objective will be to decrease the vulnerability of at-risk youth by keeping them in or reinserting them into school, as well as helping them to find gainful employment through vocational education in sectors projected to grow in the Dominican economy.

In education, USAID/Dominican Republic will work with the Ministry of Education and other private and public donors to expand USAID/Dominican Republic's Effective Schools Program that has proven successful in teaching primary school students. USAID will focus on strengthening schools in the targeted neighborhoods, while transitioning ESP to the GODR for expansion nationwide. USAID/Dominican Republic will also support a supplemental reading program in targeted neighborhoods to improve basic reading skills. Finally, USAID/Dominican Republic will promote inclusion by working with the Ministry of Education to strengthen its capacity to incorporate students with disabilities into the public schools.

USAID/Dominican Republic will also engage at the systemic level with the Ministry of Education through the USAID/Dominican Republic-sponsored Dominican Initiative for Quality Education (IDEC) that promotes transparency, accountability, and professionalism in the Ministry of Education. Assistance to the Ministry of Education in relation to implementation of IDEC recommendations may include strengthening their planning and teacher training capacity. IDEC assistance may also include continued support to the coalition of civil society and private sector organizations so they continue to provide oversight, independent analysis, and advocacy for education reform.

In reform of the criminal justice system, support will be provided to the GODR to implement key police reforms and improve prosecutorial services. Specifically, USAID/Dominican Republic will provide training and technical assistance to strengthen the transparency, accountability, professionalism and the overall institutional capacity of the GODR Office of the Attorney General and the National Police. Strengthening these key criminal justice institutions will increase the police's capacity to respond to criminal activity in a manner that is respectful of citizens' rights, collect evidence and complete quality investigations, and improve the public prosecutors' capacity to successfully prosecute criminal cases and thereby prevent and reduce crime.

USAID/Dominican Republic will also provide training and technical assistance to select NGOs who participated in the formulation and review of the GODR's National Citizen Security Plan and who provided key input into the pending Police Reform Law. Continued participation of these civil society organizations in GODR deliberations and decision-making will ensure the protection of human rights, while strengthening police and judicial performance.

The combination of systemic improvements in the judicial system and offering youth and at-risk youth a better education and more opportunities to find gainful, licit employment, should lead to a drop in crime in these targeted neighborhoods, create an improved sense of citizen security, and increase confidence in the judicial system and the police.

At the end of the five year strategy, under this Development Objective, USAID/Dominican Republic interventions will:

1. Help more than 80,000 youth aged 11-24 to finish school, get vocational training, find jobs, and develop better life skills;
2. Help 100,000 primary school students to read;
3. Reduce teen pregnancy and gang membership in targeted neighborhoods;
4. Establish six new community justice houses which will provide 125,000 poor people in marginalized urban neighborhoods with improved access to justice services, including Alternative Dispute Resolution (ADR) and conflict mediation;
5. Counsel 60,000 at-risk youth on HIV prevention and sexual and reproductive health;
6. Improve caseload management in the Attorney General's Office; and
7. Help implement reforms in both the National Police and the Attorney General's Office.

Vulnerable Populations

Special consideration will be taken to include vulnerable groups, including people with disabilities, LGBTs, those of Haitian descent, and women and girls, in the design and implementation of these activities. In terms of persons with disabilities, most schools in the Dominican Republic are not physically accessible to students with disabilities. Most children who are deaf or blind either attend special schools, or they don't attend school at all, because teachers in the regular public schools are not trained in how to teach them. A UNESCO study, published in December 2012, reported that 70 percent of children with a disability are currently not in school. Promoting inclusiveness in the education system will be an integral part of USAID/Dominican Republic's education programming and, where warranted, special programs will be funded to ensure that education is, truly, for all.

Gender Based Violence

Of particular concern is the rate of femicide. In 2000, there were 118 femicides. Over the eight year period from 2005 to 2012, femicides fluctuated between a 2006 low of 173 and a 2011 high of 233. In 2012, it decreased to 196. Women face particular challenges when they need to seek protection under the law and therefore, addressing GBV is particularly important to achievement of objectives under crime prevention. In the criminal justice sector, there are many areas where gender issues need to be specifically addressed.

The process for reporting, investigating and prosecuting GBV cases is fraught with discrimination and often re-victimizes the women pressing charges. Women frequently have to travel from rural areas to Santo Domingo to report and prosecute their cases. Cases that are sent back to the provinces for prosecution often collapse before they reach the court due to administrative technicalities or lack of interest and sensitivity of local officials to follow through.

Second, there is no national level electronic database for tracking and monitoring cases or identifying repeat offenders of GBV, a problem that often allows repeat offenders to go free. A protocol was established in the Attorney General's Office in 2012, based on Law 24-97 (Criminalization of Intra-familiar Violence and Violence against Women) for treatment of cases on intra-familiar and domestic violence against women, that requires that GBV cases be expedited. The Attorney General has imposed sanctions on prosecutors when they have not complied with prescribed timelines.

The Attorney General has also established a new network of prosecutors that work exclusively on gender violence cases, creating 17 integrated gender and interfamily violence and sexual crime units as of June, 2013.[27] These units have specialized staff, including social workers, psychologists, and attorneys, to address victims' needs. This capacity has been replicated by the Dominican National Police (DNP) which has established specialized gender and family violence units to improve Dominican law enforcement in this area. In the courts, the Gender Committee of the Courts has trained sitting judges and now includes this training as part of the basic curriculum in the judicial training centers for those entering the justice system.

To address GBV, USAID/Dominican Republic will work with the Attorney General, the National Police, and other judicial entities to improve processing and prosecution of GBV cases, improve case coordination in the criminal justice sector between the police, prosecutors, and judges, and work with the Ministry of Health to refer patients to the criminal justice system who may be victims of GBV. At the community level, USAID/Dominican Republic will expand the community justice house network services to explicitly include staff trained to properly handle and effectively prosecute GBV and domestic violence offenses.

Intermediate Result 1.1: Youth Involvement in Criminal Activities Reduced
Indicator:
- Number of youth arrests

To reduce the number of youth involved in criminal activities, the most at-risk youth will be targeted, particularly those who have one or more of the following characteristics: 1) come from socially or economically-disadvantaged households or communities; 2) are school dropouts or are one or more years behind in school; or 3) belong to communities plagued by high levels of crime, drug use and/or trafficking, youth violence, high pregnancy rates, and/or gangs. Youth in the Dominican Republic are subject to multiple forms of risky behavior. Some of these factors, including unemployment, may be partly outside their control. Others, however, are within their control, such as dropping out of school, becoming pregnant, or becoming a gang member. These risk factors contribute to youth's susceptibility to becoming involved in or victims of criminal activities.

Sub-IR 1.1.1: Economic Vulnerabilities of At Risk Youth Decreased
Indicators:
- Number of vocational training program graduates employed
- Number of students enrolled in primary or secondary schools and/or equivalent non-school-based settings

---

[27] "Procuraduría Inaugura nuevo Centro." *ElDia.com.do*. N.p., 28 June 2013. Web. 30 June 2013.

The World Bank 2006 Poverty Assessment argues that one of the five principal explanations for continuing high levels of inequality and poverty in the Dominican Republic is low labor productivity, caused by failure of the education system to impart the minimal skills required by the labor market.[28] Youth leave school lacking the skills to search for a job, an understanding of what employment opportunities are available, and the knowledge and skills required to attain the jobs they want. Another potential obstacle to at-risk youth finding jobs is that finding a job is often based on social connections; which most youth from marginal neighborhoods do not have. Employers may also be reluctant to hire youth, particularly from poor communities. Thus, working with the GODR and the private sector to develop programs and identify employment opportunities for at-risk youth is crucial for providing an alternative to criminal activity.

The Dominican Republic has a high dropout rate, and boys tend to drop out at a higher rate than girls, making boys more susceptible to crime and gang membership.[29] In a 2001 study conducted in the Dominican Republic, focus groups revealed that students did not perceive significant income returns for completing secondary school. However, when parents and students were given data demonstrating an 8 percent income return for every additional year they stayed in school, children stayed in school more years, and the greatest improvements in school retention were made by the poorest students.[30] Thus, ensuring parents and students understand more fully the benefits of staying in school can have a positive effect on school retention rates.

A major cause of crime in the Dominican Republic is the limited number of jobs for youth, especially those who come from low-income families. In the Dominican Republic, 34 percent of youth are neither working nor in school. According to a Central Bank survey in 2011, 30 percent of Dominicans age 18-29 were unemployed. Many young Dominicans lack the necessary skills and education to obtain employment and earn a living, which is a result of both the poor quality of education and the fact that many young Dominicans drop out of school.[31] USAID/Dominican Republic presumes that, if given the opportunity, and if the income earned was relatively equal, at-risk youth would choose legal employment over involvement in illegal income-earning activities.

USAID/Dominican Republic, through the *Alerta Joven* program, has conducted a labor market survey to identify labor needs in the targeted communities and in the overall economy. This program begins by identifying what jobs are available or will be created in the private and public sectors and then works backwards through the 'supply chain' to design vocational education programs that satisfy market demand for specific labor shortages.

In a 2012 study conducted by four local organizations, 10 sectors have been specifically identified for their overall projected growth rate through 2020 and their ability to absorb new labor force entrants, particularly youth. These sectors include cinematography, telecommunications, pharmaceuticals, technology, manufacturing, construction, mining and electricity. This study was subsequently ground-truthed with three industry associations, including AMCHAM/DR. These assessments confirm that

---

[28] Dominican Republic Poverty Assessment, 2006.
http://web.worldbank.org/WBSITE/EXTERNAL/COUNTRIES/LACEXT/0,,contentMDK:21092870~pagePK:146736~piPK:146830~theSitePK:258554,00.html
[29] Final Report: DR Cross-Sectoral Youth Assessment, 2010
[30] Jensen, Robert "The Perceived Returns to Education and the Demand for Schooling" The Quarterly Journal of Economics, 2010
[31] "El 34% Abandona las Aulas y no Trabaja, en RD" El Dia Newspaper, November 8, 2012

businesses are creating jobs, particularly at the technical level, but they cannot find qualified people to fill these jobs.

Private sector businesses have also been investing their own time and money training/retraining people who have graduated from technical/vocational education schools, but still are not qualified to fill their technical positions. For example, Caterpillar, (Implementos y Maquinarias), is funding its own vocational program because it cannot find enough skilled diesel mechanics. The Vicini Group, the largest sugar producer in the Dominican Republic, is planning to replicate the Caterpiller model, again with its own funds, to supply its labor needs.

Much emphasis has been placed on training Dominicans for professional careers, resulting in a surplus of doctors and lawyers, but a shortage of skilled technicians. Areas where youth may have opportunities to find jobs include: call centers, trades (electricians, plumbers), nursing, community-based tourism, farming, and mining. Call centers alone are creating 6,000 new jobs a year, but they are having difficulty finding Dominicans who have sufficient command of English.

Accordingly, USAID/Dominican Republic will fund a range of activities to keep young people in school or motivate them to return to school. These activities can include intense remedial education programs that allow students to catch up on academic skills so they can continue with their formal schooling at an age appropriate level and providing parents and students with data that demonstrates the increased income their children will earn if they stay in school. It would also include working in concert with community leaders, parents and school officials to identify students who are still in school, but for whatever reason are struggling, and helping them to overcome their challenges so they don't drop out; and providing young people and parents with information on the very real dangers of becoming involved in illicit activities.

In the area of vocational education, USAID/Dominican Republic will work in concert with other donors, the private sector, universities and NGOs to develop a comprehensive and effective vocational education and life skills program for youth who have already dropped out of formal education institutions and are not likely or interested in returning to school. USAID/Dominican Republic will help them develop their marketable skills through workforce development programs, help place them in full-time jobs in the private and public sector, and provide them with on-going counseling. USAID/Dominican Republic will thus help prevent crime by building a solid evidence base of "what works" and "what does not work" when it comes to job training and placement for at-risk youth.

Sub-IR 1.1.2: Social Vulnerabilities of At Risk Youth Decreased
Indicators:
* Teenage pregnancy rates in targeted areas
* Number of youth in targeted communities that are members of a gang

Complicating youth unemployment are the social factors that make at-risk youth more vulnerable, including teenage pregnancy and gang membership.

Teenage pregnancy is on the rise. In a July 12, 2013 news article, the UN Population Fund (UNFPA) stated that the teenage pregnancy rate for the Dominican Republic in 2012 was 22.1 percent, up from

19 percent in 2011 and 14.8 percent in 2007.[32] UNFPA added that 50 percent of the adolescents surveyed were not using any family planning methods. The Ministry of Women currently seeks to reduce the teen pregnancy rate from 22.1% to 18% as teen pregnancy has deleterious long-term effects, often forcing girls to interrupt their studies, hindering their academic, personal and social development, thus limiting their future job opportunities and earning potential.

A major reason why girls drop out of school, usually around the 8th grade, is because they become pregnant. In 2004, 18 percent of females aged 14 to17 years cited pregnancy as the reason they left school. Overall, forty percent of Dominican girls were married by age 18 in 2012.[33] The 2007 Demographic Health Survey revealed that among women who received four years or less of primary education, 43.8 percent became pregnant during their teenage years, compared to 13.3 percent among women who completed secondary or higher education. Clearly, keeping girls in school will help stem the rise in teenage pregnancy and the negative effects it has on the health and welfare of both the mother and the child. Early sexual debut, especially among females in rural areas and those who do not complete primary school, is also a significant issue related to higher incidences of both teen pregnancy and HIV.[34] The current public school curriculum gives limited attention to gender issues and sexual and reproductive health, and traditional teaching approaches tend to reinforce gender stereotypes, including a lack of equity in responsibility for sexual activity that largely falls on girls to *"cuidarse"* (take care of themselves).

Membership in gangs is also on the rise. The 2012 LAPOP survey ranked the Dominican Republic first of all Latin American countries, even higher than Honduras, in reporting their neighborhoods were affected by gangs, 48.6 percent in the Dominican Republic versus 29.6 percent in Honduras. This finding may reflect the fact that Dominicans may use a different definition of what constitutes a 'gang' than people in other countries. Of the 63 percent of youth living in urban areas, those living in poor, crime-ridden neighborhoods are at highest risk of becoming part of a criminal gang. For many youth, membership in gangs provides the social support network they have not found elsewhere, due to the exclusion they face by the wider Dominican society.

USAID/Dominican Republic will work with partners, including the GODR, NGOs, other donors, the private sector, municipal and central governments, churches, and community organizations to replicate programs which have demonstrated impact in reducing teen pregnancy and gang membership. This may include teenager peer to peer counseling and working with former gang members in order to effectively 'reach' our target audience.

Intermediate Result 1.2: Increased Reading Skills of Primary School Students in Targeted Areas
Indicators:
- Number of students with improved reading scores
- Proportion of students who, by the end of primary school, are able to read

One of the Dominican Republic's fundamental development challenges is the failure to provide its children with a quality public education. The Dominican Republic ranked 143rd out of 144 countries surveyed in terms of quality of primary education, according to the World Economic Forum 2012-2013 Global Competitiveness Report.

---

[32] Dominicana en Cifras 2012. Page 40. Oficina Nacional de Estadística
[33] http://www.unfpa.org/webdav/site/global/shared/swp/2012/EN_SWOP2012_Report.pdf
[34] DHS

In 2011, according to World Bank World Development Indicators[35], 89.4 percent of primary school aged children are enrolled in primary school in the Dominican Republic, as compared to 94 percent of children in similar income countries. In the Dominican Republic, the typical school day is only 2 hours and 40 minutes long, and although by law, students should receive 1,000 hours of class per year, in reality they only receive 500. In public schools with 500 students or more (accounting for 68 percent of total enrollment in public schools), the student-teacher ratio is 78:1. Such overcrowding severely hampers teachers' capacity to address individual student needs. In addition to overcrowding, poor learning outcomes contribute to high repetition and drop-out rates, resulting in more delayed and over-age students in each successive grade. Completion of 8th grade among those that ever entered school remains low, despite considerable improvements from 23 percent in 1988 to 53 percent in 1998 to 64 percent for boys and 74 percent for girls in 2007.[36]

Similar to patterns observed throughout the Caribbean, the average educational achievement for girls is higher than boys.[37] As a result of lower education levels, male youth are disproportionately likely to be illiterate, constituting 59 and 69 percent of those unable to read and write, respectively, depending on the age group.[38]

Low primary school completion and attainment rates and low secondary school enrollment rates are also significant risk factors for participation in gangs and drug trafficking.[39] Considerable research now shows that strengthening early grade reading keeps young people in school[40] and lays the foundation necessary for future economic success and social mobility.[41] Thus, early grade reading is an important contributing factor to reducing the risk of engagement in violent or criminal behavior later in life.[42]

Not surprisingly, in terms of student achievement outcomes, the Dominican Republic's education outcomes are well below the expected level for a middle-income country. The 2006 Programme for International Student Assessment revealed that only 26 percent of Dominican students in mathematics, 46 percent in reading, and 50 percent in science achieved a level one, the minimum standard of learning that every student should achieve. Only one out of every 240 Dominican students was able to achieve the average score of students in Organization for Economic Co-operation and Development countries. To reinforce this finding, in the 2008 Second Regional Comparative and Explanatory Study (SERCE), the Dominican Republic scored the lowest of 16 Latin American countries in 3rd and 6th grade math, reading and natural science. The Autonomous University of Santo Domingo reported in

[35] World Development Indicators, found at http://data.worldbank.org/indicator/SE.PRM.NENR/countries/DO-XJ-XT?display=graph

[36] USAID/Dominican Republic. Dominican Republic Cross Sectoral Youth Assessment, 2010.

[37] In 2008-09, primary education enrollment was 89%, while secondary enrollment is dramatically lower at 50% (Source: MINERD, 2010: *Boletín de Indicadores: Año Lectivo 20082009*). For every 100 boys enrolled in primary, secondary and university and technical schools there are 93, 127 and 159 females enrolled respectively (Source: Gender Assessment).

[38] Central Bank: National Labor Force Survey Database, 2nd Semester 2008

[39] McClean Hilker, Linsday, and Erika Fraser. *Youth Exclusion, Violence, Conflict, and Fragile States.* Report prepared for DFID's Equity and Rights Team. Social Development Direct, 2009.

[40] Patrinos, H.A. and Velez, E. (2009). "Costs and benefits of bilingual education in Guatemala: A partial analysis." *International Journal of Educational Development* 29(6): 594-598.

[41] Hanushek, E. and L. Woessmann. Do Better Schools Lead To More Growth? Cognitive Skills, Economic Outcomes, and Causation. NBER Working Paper 14633. National Bureau of Economic Research, 2009.

[42] Cunningham, Wendy, et al. *Youth at Risk in Latin America and the Caribbean: Understanding the Causes, Realizing the Potential* (Washington DC: World Bank, 2008).

2011 that the average incoming student tests at a sixth grade level; meaning it takes 12 years to achieve the equivalent of a sixth grade education in the Dominican Republic.[43]

Although 88 percent of Dominican teachers are certified, a rate higher than countries like Ecuador and Costa Rica, they have not achieved similar education results. According to a 2008 Gallup study, teachers attend 92 percent of their classes, showing that teacher absenteeism is not a factor in low performance. This suggests that teachers may not have the capacity to teach their assigned subjects. A study (Gonzalez, Gonzalez, Tapia, and Dominguez 2007) showed that mathematics teachers in selected schools understood only 42.28 percent of the material they were supposed to be teaching. Although this may not be a representative sample, it does indicate serious problems with teacher training, and is consistent with another finding which showed that there was little difference between student performances in public versus private schools.

Private schools don't appear to perform any better than public schools. Results from the SERCE Study and the Latin American Laboratory for the Evaluation of the Quality of Education confirm little variance between public and private school student test results, a fact reconfirmed by a report by the Harvard Institute for International Development, which reported no statistical difference on test performance between public /private schools and urban/rural schools[44].

Lack of funding has also been part of the problem. Dominican public expenditure in education has been historically low, around 2.5 percent of the GDP. In FY 2011, civil society organizations created a Coalition for a Dignified Education. This coalition included more than 200 civil society organizations that lobbied for GODR compliance with the Education Law, which requires that four percent of GDP be allocated for education. The coalition was able to obtain a public commitment from each of the candidates in the May 2012 Presidential election to comply with the four percent requirement.

To date, USAID/Dominican Republic has focused much of its Basic Education programming on in-service teacher training, through a program implemented through the Catholic University (PUCMM) as low teacher capacity is considered the greatest contributing factor to poor student academic achievement. USAID/Dominican Republic's basic education program has demonstrated improved basic reading and mathematics skills in the first through fourth grades. Test results from USAID's Effective Schools Program in 2012 show that up to four times as many students whose teachers received one to three years of USAID/Dominican Republic training and materials support, performed at or above the minimum standard, as compared to students whose teachers were not trained through this USAID-funded program. This shows that improving the quality of instruction positively affects student performance, and that the USAID-funded model is working. In FY 2011 and 2012 USAID worked with the GODR and Dominican private and foundation partners to expand this model to more schools.

Consistent with USAID's Global Education Strategy, USAID/Dominican Republic will focus on improving reading scores. By working with the Ministry of Education and other multi-lateral and private sector donors, USAID/Dominican Republic will identify, test and scale up proven approaches

---

[43] Construyendo un Mejor Futuro para la Republica Dominicana: Herramientas para el Desarrollo, March 2011. http://www.hks.harvard.edu/var/ezp_site/storage/fckeditor/file/pdfs/centers-programs/centers/cid/growth/dominican/CID-RD_InformeTecnico.pdf
[44] ibid

to improve early grade reading. It will also actively seek partners to complement USAID-funded reading programs with materials and training in science and math. USAID/Dominican Republic will also work with these partners to create school environments that are safe and inclusive. Finally, USAID/Dominican Republic's education program will encourage parental and community involvement in encouraging special needs children to attend school, and to provide teachers with the training and materials they need in order to teach them.

Sub-IR 1.2.1 Quality of Reading Instruction Improved In Targeted Areas
Indicators:
- Proportion of primary school classrooms effectively utilizing high quality teaching and learning materials
- Time on task for reading instruction

USAID/Dominican Republic will work with the Ministry of Education to expand the Effective Schools Program approach both in scope and quality, with a specific focus on improving the reading skills of students in targeted poor neighborhoods. Piloted by USAID/Dominican Republic, the ESP program has generated learning gains among participating students that are significantly greater than non-participants, and garnered support from the private sector as well as the GODR. This will include the creation/adaptation of teaching materials and supporting teacher training to create a critical mass of trainers needed to expand the ESP program nationwide.

Sub-IR 1.2.2 Opportunities for Learning to Read Increased in Targeted Areas
Indicators:
- Number of parent and community groups supporting traditional and alternative student reading programs
- Number of extracurricular reading programs available

In addition to targeted support for teacher training and materials development, USAID will also provide research-based supplemental reading programs focused in, but not exclusive to, areas targeted by the at-risk youth Alerta Joven Program. These programs will be flexible enough to be administered by a trained teacher, technician, or aide as an afterschool program, a remedial reading program during regular school hours, or during an extended after school program. Activities will increase the number of parent and community groups supporting traditional and alternative student reading programs, and increase the number of extracurricular reading programs available to first through fourth grade students.

Intermediate Result 1.3: Criminal Justice Institutions Strengthened
Indicators:
- Time from Arrest to Trial
- Confidence in Justice System
- Number of people who receive services from community justice houses

Compared to other LAC countries, the Dominican Republic is seventh lowest in terms of citizen confidence in justice. In 2012, the AmericasBarometer survey reflected a 45.1 percent confidence in justice, lower than in Guatemala. The 2012 WEF report ranks the Dominican Republic second to last (of 144 countries globally) on quality of police services.

Poor and marginalized Dominicans have difficulty in gaining access to legal services and thus have few legal means to pursue justice or arbitrate disputes. Strengthening criminal justice institutions, in particular the Attorney General and the National Police, to better protect poor citizens who live in crime-ridden neighborhoods will improve citizen security and citizen confidence in their justice institutions.

At the community level, USAID/Dominican Republic will support expansion and strengthening of the community justice houses, where GODR prosecutors and public defenders partner with civil society, municipal officials, and private sector representatives to increase access to justice. Currently there are four community justice houses in the Dominican Republic, all started with USAID/Dominican Republic funds. They have provided access to justice to over 15,000 primarily poor families every year, 75,000 people so far. The Prosecutor's office, NGOs, and municipal officials now provide both financial and in-kind (staff and buildings) support to these community justice houses. Approximately 75 percent of current community justice house operational costs are now covered by non-USAID sources.

Sub-IR 1.3.1 Prosecutor Capacity Strengthened
Indicators:
- Number of cases prosecuted (disaggregated by type of crime, including GBV)
- Number of convictions (disaggregated by type of crime, including GBV)
- Number of Alternative Dispute Resolutions (ADRs)/binding conciliations completed (disaggregated by type of case, including GBV)

Only 5 percent of arrests in the Santo Domingo province result in conviction. USAID/Dominican Republic will strengthen the institutional capacity of the Office of the Attorney General and selected prosecutors' offices to manage criminal caseloads transparently and efficiently, coordinate investigations with the Dominican National Police, and integrate caseload tracking, administrative and operations management.

Sub-IR 1.3.2 Targeted Capacities of Dominican National Police Strengthened
Indicators:
- Citizen confidence in the national police
- Reforms implemented

Citizen confidence in the national police is low. In the 2012 LAPOP survey, only 34.9 percent of the population had confidence in the police, the third lowest rating of any LAC country, and a significant decrease from the 2008 confidence level of 46.6 percent. Low public confidence in police is exacerbated by the organizational and institutional weakness of the Dominican National Police (DNP).

USAID/Dominican Republic assistance will focus on improving the DNP's strategic planning skills, their ability to recruit, train, and evaluate staff performance in a transparent and objective fashion, and effectively assign personnel to accomplish its mission. USAID/Dominican Republic assistance will also strengthen the DNP's capacity to conduct internal investigations and administer disciplinary action. Increasing the DNP's transparency in budget management and procurement, and improving compliance with freedom of information to the public are also important aspects of institutional strengthening designed to increase citizen confidence in the police. It is expected that improved transparency and accountability within the DNP – both in its financial and administrative operations, as well as in its engagement with citizens – will improve both public confidence in the national police as well as its effectiveness in preventing crime, arresting criminals when crimes do occur, effectively investigating crimes, and improving citizen security.

Policy Dialogue

Policy dialogue with the Dominican Office of the President, Attorney General, and Congress will play a key role in the accomplishment of CDCS justice and citizen security goals. USAID will work closely with these actors to strengthen the legal framework for citizen security and police reform, and ensure GODR ownership and funding of critical access to justice and crime prevention initiatives such as the Community Justice House program ("Casa de Justicia"). Policy dialogue at this level will also be critical to ensuring that youth and human development components of the Mission's citizen security agenda are met. In this regard, USAID/Dominican Republic will engage with the Ministry of Education and the private sector to adopt the Effective Schools model nationwide, promote nationwide student testing, increase education opportunities for at risk youth and students with special needs, and promote tolerance and creation of a safe environment for learning for all in the schools. USAID/Dominican Republic will also work closely with the Ministry of Youth to create public awareness of Youth Law 49-00 and to promote public policies that specifically respond to the needs of Dominican youth.

Partnerships

1. GODR

On March 7, 2013 the GODR adopted a national strategy for citizen security and is reallocating funds within the national budget to implement this strategy. The plan is a holistic approach to citizen security, which includes police reform, judicial reform, crime prevention, and education. A new national police reform law has also been introduced to Congress, designed to restructure and strengthen the DNP to transform it into a modern and professional institution. Chief priorities of the GODR's national police reform effort include:
- The creation and adoption of a merit-based recruitment and career system
- Strengthening the transparency and independence of internal affairs and disciplinary functions
- Integrating DNP budget and procurement functions into national financial management systems
- Rightsizing the overall DNP workforce and eliminating moonlighting by DNP officers as private security guards, drivers, and other non-sanctioned positions.
- Passage of the Organic Law for the National Police.

In efforts to represent the rights and serve the needs of Dominican citizens directly, the Attorney General and National Prosecutor's Office have committed its own staff and resources to assign a GODR prosecutor to each USAID/Dominican Republic-funded Community Justice House. These resources have been matched by the national public defender's office, as well as the provision of office space by municipal authorities. Prosecutors and public defenders work collaboratively in each venue to provide criminal justice guidance referral, as well as alternative dispute resolution services to more than 15,000 people annually. In collaboration with local women's advocacy and health organizations,

USAID also offers gender violence guidance and referral support in Santiago based on high rates of GBV and family violence reported in the region.

Implemented under the legal and policy oversight of the GODR Supreme Court of Justice, four USAID-supported community justice houses operate in Santo Domingo, La Vega and Santiago. During CDCS implementation, USAID will expand the overall number of community justice houses operating in the Dominican Republic to 10, and deepen its support for GBV prevention and response efforts. USAID will also increase the availability of family and gender violence counseling services available via the community justice houses to ensure coverage in areas of greatest need, and strengthen the institutional and organizational capacity of national and provincial prosecutors to investigate and combat gender crimes.

In the area of vocational education, the Dominican government, through Ministries including the Ministry of Youth, is already investing its own resources in training youth, partnering with a local call center cluster to co-fund English language training, sending 1,200 students to the U.S. for renewable energy training, training nurses in the U.S., and creating a $500,000 microcredit fund for youth farmers.

In education, the Ministry of Education has expressed interest in expanding USAID/Dominican Republic's Effective Schools Program and is already working with the Inter-American Development Bank and the INICIA Foundation to do so. USAID/Dominican Republic will also work with the Ministry to produce accessible reading and teaching materials that will focus on basic literacy skills so that all students, including those with learning challenges, have an opportunity to learn.

The Medina administration has also made reducing violence against women a priority. In November 2012, a nationwide campaign was launched against GBV. The Armed Forces, National Police, Tourist Police, schools, Vice President, civil society, media, donors, and the private sector all coordinated efforts. The reduction in femicides in 2012 could, in part, be attributed to this comprehensive campaign. USAID/Dominican Republic will work closely with the Attorney General, the National Police, National Prosecutors Office, and civil society to further advance this effort and related GBV prevention and response efforts.

2. Donors

UNDP, the Spanish Cooperation Agency, the Inter-American Development Bank and USAID/Dominican Republic, along with civil society organizations have coalesced and are working in concert to encourage police reform. UNDP is supporting the establishment of a 911 emergency response system, the Spanish Cooperation Agency is training police, and the IDB has performed an assessment of citizen security. The Government of Colombia and the Colombian National Police have also been working with their Dominican police counterparts on police reform. South-South cooperation will be encouraged.

Significant support to the GODR for youth activities has come from the World Bank (WB) and the IDB. Both the WB and the IDB also support *Solidaridad*, a conditional cash transfer program that provides cash transfers to poor households if families invest more in education, health, and nutrition.

USAID/Dominican Republic works with key donors such as the World Bank, the European Union, the Spanish Cooperation Agency, UNICEF and the IDB on both strengthening civil society and establishing a workplan for education reform and improvement. The WB also supports *Juventud y Empleo*, a vocational training program that incorporates life skills training and internships to provide youth with marketable job skills. The European Union and the Spanish Cooperation Agency have provided technical support in helping undocumented youth obtain the documents needed for school enrollment and employment.

The IDB also is funding a pilot program to extend the school day. They are interested in working with USAID/Dominican Republic to use the Early Grade Reading Assessment (EGRA), developed for the Dominican Republic by USAID in the Fall of 2012, as a means of measuring gains in literacy by the participating students. USAID/Dominican Republic will work with the IDB and the MOE to adopt an EGRA or similar assessment that will be able to be used to measure reading improvements.

3. *Private Sector and Civil Society*

The private sector has already been supporting judicial and police reform, through groups such as the Association of Young Entrepreneurs, the National Council of Businessmen and the Justice and Institutionality Foundation. They have established a coalition of civil society and private sector actors to support reform of the National Police and to improve citizen security.

The private sector, churches, and NGOs all support vocational training. Both the Salesian and Jesuit orders support technical institutes focused on providing training to at-risk youth. The Americas Technological Institute provides computer and language programs designed for at-risk youth. Local partners such as ENTRENA support vocational and remedial education programs.

The INICIA Foundation has the express purpose of improving public education in the Dominican Republic. INICIA has already been financially supporting expansion of the USAID/Dominican Republic-funded Effective Schools Program to 50 additional schools. USAID/Dominican Republic will be exploring the possibility of establishing a more formal alliance with INICIA to further expand the breadth, depth, and impact of the Effective Schools Program. The American Chamber of Commerce of the Dominican Republic has been implementing a program to promote private sector investment in education. The program provides technical and financial assistance to private sector institutions in their individual efforts to support Dominican public primary education.

Development Objective 2: Increased Resilience of People to the Impact of Climate Change
Indicator:

- Climate change vulnerability index of target geographic areas and target populations/government entities

The Dominican Republic, as a small island nation, is extremely vulnerable to Global Climate Change (GCC). According to the Germanwatch 2013 Climate Risk Index, over the last twenty years, the Dominican Republic has been the tenth most affected country in the world by weather events (fourth in Latin America and the Caribbean). This vulnerability will only worsen as climate change continues to bring more extreme storms, landslides, floods, and droughts, as well as slower climate change effects, such as sea level rise and a gradual reduction in water quality and quantity.

This vulnerability to GCC has a profound impact on the strategy's goal of improving citizen security. In the Dominican Republic, climate change is already negatively impacting the stability of water supply and critical coastal resources important for disaster risk reduction and economic growth, with disproportionate effects on vulnerable populations and the tourism industry. Numerous global studies, including a 2007 Climate Change and National Security study [45] and a 2009 International Institute for Sustainable Development report, have found that reduced water supply, unpredictable weather patterns, population migration induced by sea level rise, and increased disease burden from cumulative climate impacts "threaten to increase poverty and overwhelm the capacity of governments to meet the basic needs of their people. Fundamentally this could mean more fragile and failed states."[46]

In the largest Dominican cities, Santo Domingo and Santiago, climate change will bring more intense storms and increase flooding risk, endangering the lives and livelihoods of the hundreds of thousands of urban poor living illegally along the cities' riverbanks and negatively impacting already tenuous access to potable water. In Santo Domingo, conservative estimates by the municipality put 200,000 people, or 20 percent of its population, in slum neighborhoods, most of which are located in flood- and landslide-prone areas along the Ozama and Isabel Rivers. In Santiago, 2010 estimates of households living below the poverty line rose 13 percent over ten years, to 12.4 percent of total households, many of which also live in vulnerable urban zones along the Yaque del Norte River. Focusing GCC assistance geographically in the same communities where DO 1 activities will be implemented should increase synergy between these two programs and maximize benefits for the most vulnerable populations.

In terms of potable water, the Dominican Republic is already experiencing deteriorating access to potable water, particularly in these same vulnerable urban areas. As climate change brings heavier rains and more prolonged dry spells, current deficiencies in water service delivery will be more pronounced. These systemic deficiencies are exacerbated by the fact that in Santo Domingo roughly 55 percent of piped water is lost in distribution through leakage or illegal connections.[47]

---

[45] Busby, Joshua W. "Climate Change and National Security." November 2007: http://www.cfr.org/climate-change/climate-change-national-security/p14862

[46] Brown, Oli. Crawford, Alec. "Battling the Elements: The Security Threat of Climate Change." International Institute for Sustainable Development, December 2009: http://www.iisd.org/pdf/2009/COP15_Commentary_Battling_the_Elements_Oli_Alec.pdf

[47] Herrera-Miniño, Fabio R. "Las fugas y presas afectan el agua de la capital. " HOY newspaper March 20, 2013: http://www.hoy.com.do/opiniones/2013/3/20/472306/print

Vulnerable coastal populations and tourism investments are also threatened by GCC impacts. The Global Flood Map predicts that with a one meter rise in sea level (the middle of the range predicted by the end of the century), almost 200,000 people in the Dominican Republic would be permanently flooded[48]. The number of people potentially affected by this rise in sea level does not take into account that 76 percent of the population growth forecasted between 2010 and 2020 is expected to occur in coastal provinces.[49]

In areas that depend on groundwater supplies for potable water, such as the Southeast region, sea level rise will lead to groundwater salinization. USAID/Dominican Republic funded a 2013 climate change vulnerability assessment, which also highlights that unplanned tourism development in several key coastal communities has drained underground aquifers and increased salt water intrusion, threatening the stability of the drinking water supply. This could negatively impact the sustainability of current tourism facilities and slow the future development of the tourism industry. This could also negatively impact the rate of job creation in the tourism industry, a sector which could potentially absorb a lot of new labor entrants.

Another major threat to coastal communities and the tourism industry is the continued loss of coral reefs, mangroves, and wetlands that protect its 1,600 km of beach from storm surges. According to the African and Latin American Resilience to Climate Change assessment, virtually all of the Dominican Republic's critical marine resources are at risk and 70-90 percent of coral reefs are already dead.[50] Both non-climate stressors (such as industrial and agricultural pollution, and land clearing/wetland elimination for tourism development) and climate stressors (such as increased water temperature and acidity) are degrading this important "blue infrastructure."

In 2010, the World Resources Institute determined that the country is losing, on average, a half meter of beach per year, which could directly lead to the loss of $52-100 million worth of private sector investments already made in beachfront tourism facilities.[51] This is particularly significant, given that "beach quality" has been cited as the main reason for visiting the Dominican Republic by more than a quarter of tourists.[52] Not only does this put the homes and lives of people in Santo Domingo and other coastal communities at risk, but it poses yet another significant threat to tourism.

Specifically, the strategy will develop and improve municipal land use planning processes to integrate climate change information into the decision-making process at the municipal level, and increase the adoption of adaptation measures, with a particular focus on protecting water resources and reducing disaster risks in Santo Domingo and Santiago. These urban areas are home to a majority of the Dominican population and reflect the Mission's concentration on reducing the vulnerability of the most marginalized populations. The GCC component of this strategy will also work in select coastal cities which are threatened by GCC impacts.

---

[48] Global Food Map Dominican Republic: http://globalfloodmap.org/Dominican_Republic accessed 2013
[49] Office of National Statistics, Department of Demographic, Social, and Cultural Statistics
[50] Climate Change Vulnerability Assessment of the Dominican Republic, ARCC-USAID, August, 2013.
[51] Coastal Capital: Economic Valuation of Coral Reefs in the Dominican Republic, WRI, Wielgus, Jeffrey. Cooper, Emily. Torres, Rubén. Burke, Lauretta. April 2010: http://www.wri.org/publication/coastal-capital-dominican-republic
[52] Wielgus, J., E. Cooper, R. Torres and L. Burke. 2010. Coastal Capital: Dominican Republic. Case studies on the economic value of coastal ecosystems in the Dominican Republic. Working Paper. Washington, DC: World Resources Institute: http://www.wri.org/coastal-capital

At the end of this five year strategy, USAID/Dominican Republic interventions will have produced the following results:

1. Four municipalities will have incorporated climate change into land use plans.
2. Targeted vulnerable populations will have access to climate information, the knowledge to interpret that information, and the capacity to translate the information into appropriate and effective risk-reducing measures.
3. Resources, such as watersheds, coastal ecosystems, and specific urban communities will have reduced damage from more frequent severe storms as well as the slower onset effects of climate change, such as changes in rainfall.
4. Vulnerable populations will be better protected from climate change impacts and will have become active participants in their local land use planning processes, contributing to creating a more inclusive and democratic Dominican Republic.

Vulnerable Populations

The poor, women, people with disabilities, and members of the LGBT community often are not participants included in planning decisions at the local level. Although more specific concerns relating to gender are summarized below, many of these same gender exclusionary practices apply equally to poor people, people with disabilities, and the LGBT community. The exclusionary practices will be explicitly addressed during implementation of GCC programs.

In both urban and coastal cities and towns, the link between climate change and citizen security is disproportionately acute for socially and economically disadvantaged women. A 2008 UNFP/UN-INSTRAW study on the effect of Hurricane Noel on vulnerable populations in the Dominican Republic found that "sexual violence, including sexual abuse, increased significantly"[53] after the hurricane hit. The same phenomenon unfortunately occurred most recently in Haiti after the 2010 earthquake. A New York University School of Law study found that 70 percent of people in internally displaced person camps in Port-au-Prince were more worried about sexual violence after the earthquake than before.

Given that women in many cases make household decisions differently, occupy different parts of economic value chains, and may have different (often lower) levels of economic mobility, the lack of female representation in planning processes means that their unique needs are not incorporated into decisions. A UNDP study[54] on enhancing gender visibility in climate change in the Dominican Republic found that women generally had less access to key weather-related information, such as early warnings. Moreover, the roughly 35 percent of households headed by women tend to be more vulnerable to poverty, with less access to healthcare, education, and financial tools[55], all of which further suppresses a family's ability to recover physically and economically from a disaster.

---

[53] UNFP/UN-INSTRAW (2008). "Evaluación rápida sobre salud sexual y reproductiva, violencia contra las mujeres y situación de las personas vulnerables afectadas por la tormenta Noel en la Republica Dominicana."

[54] UNDP. Enhancing Gender Visibility in Disaster Risk Management and Climate Change in the Caribbean. Country Assessment Report for the Dominican Republic. 2009

[55] Social Institutions & Gender Index Dominican Republic: http://genderindex.org/country/dominican-republic

Intermediate Result 2.1: Land Use Planning Reduces Negative Impact from Climate Change
Indicator:
- Number of adaptation strategies in municipal plans as a result of USAID-supported land use planning processes.

With proper land use planning, manmade or natural infrastructure can be properly sited and prioritized to protect vulnerable populations and coastal communities from increased risk of flooding from sea level rise and storm surge. Additionally, land use planning is a critical tool for municipalities to manage and protect human life and property (public and private), and basic infrastructure. Since 2012, USAID/Dominican Republic has been supporting fast-growing coastal tourist towns, such as Samaná-Las Terrenas and Bayahibe, to improve their land use planning and zoning capacity in order to address rapidly growing development and resource pressures related to the tourism industry. In Samaná Province, the new land use planning process has identified various downstream flooding risks from upstream watershed degradation and lack of waste management; risks that will be compounded by climate change. USAID/Dominican Republic has also begun supporting reforestation of watersheds and restoration of mangroves to protect vulnerable populations in high priority areas.

USAID/Dominican Republic's work in Samaná Province has also highlighted the need for up-to-date and reliable climate information. Currently, climate change information generated at the Caribbean regional and national levels does not effectively flow to local governments and institutions. Moreover, available information is often not appropriate or understandable given institutional, technical, and human capacity issues and the different needs of local versus national governments.

Sub-IR 2.1.1: Capacity of Municipalities to Develop and Implement Participatory Land Use Plans Increased
Indicator:
- Number of laws, policies, strategies, plans, agreements, or regulations addressing climate change and/or biodiversity conservation officially proposed or adopted.

Although land use planning processes do not yet exist for most municipalities, there are municipal models inside and outside of the Dominican Republic that USAID/Dominican Republic will utilize to develop local capacity. USAID/Dominican Republic will help improve land use planning in a few key urban areas, such as Santo Domingo-National District, Santiago, and selected coastal tourist towns. This will build on work by other organizations, such as the Federation of Municipalities (FEDOMU), which is helping dozens of municipalities to complete robust municipal development plans.[56] There are also a few coastal cities, such as Bayahibe, Samaná, Monte Cristi, and Puerto Plata, where USAID/Dominican Republic can build on strong partnerships already forged between the private sector, central and municipal governments, and NGOs.

USAID/Dominican Republic will also emphasize the development of new coalitions and strengthen existing ones between the municipalities, the central government, civil society, and the private sector.

---

[56] FEDOMU Proyecto Planifica: http://www.proyectoplanifica.org/tag/fedomu

Sub-IR 2.1.2: Capacity of Selected Public Institutions to Integrate Climate Change Information into Planning Processes Increased

Indicator:

- Number of municipal plans that integrate climate information into analysis and priorities

As stated previously, municipalities need GCC information that is generated and packaged according to their specific needs. For example, municipalities need a variety of inputs to understand flood risk, such as meteorological data from the National Meteorology Office (ONAMET) and hydrological data from the National Institute for Hydrological Resources (INDHRI) in a format that fits into their GIS and/or other existing data analysis systems.

This strategy will help key national organizations, such as ONAMET and INDHRI, to improve data quality standards, increase data analysis/climate projection capacity, and ensure that climate information is provided in a timely fashion and meets user needs. This strategy will also strengthen information flows between and among municipalities, ONAMET, the National Climate Change Council, FEDOMU, INDHRI, local NGOs, producer associations, and other donors.

Partnerships will also be strengthened throughout the Caribbean by leveraging the work being done by the Caribbean Institute for Meteorology and Hydrology, the University of the West Indies, and the Caribbean Community Climate Change Center. These groups generate a significant amount of climate information and analysis that can be better linked to national and local institutions in the Dominican Republic.

Lastly, USAID/Dominican Republic has identified major climate information gaps and through this strategy, will develop weather forecasts and climate analysis tailored specifically for particular end users, such as small farmers.

After five years, as a result of these efforts, selected municipalities will have a cadre of trained land use planners. These land use planners will have access to relevant and appropriate climate information. They will have adopted land use plans that incorporate climate change risks, prioritize actions to manage those risks, and are implementing that plan. Finally, climate information will flow more smoothly and quickly from international to national to sub-national levels to individual users, such as farmers and producer associations.

Intermediate Result 2.2: Climate-Related Risk Reduction Measures Implemented

Indicator:

- Number of people and institutions with increased capacity to adapt to the impacts of climate variability and change

Since 2011, USAID/Dominican Republic has been supporting the implementation of climate change adaptation measures, such as improved watershed management in the Yaque del Norte watershed near Santiago, mangrove restoration in Samaná, coral reef restoration in Bayahibe, and improved on-farm management of water in major agricultural production zones. USAID/Dominican Republic has also been replicating the success of some Dominican-led adaptation measures. For example, Santiago is currently experimenting with a water fund in nearby Jarabacoa, where the Ministry of Environment, together with a hydroelectric firm, have created a payment for ecological services program where coffee farmers are paid $50 to $70/hectare to more sustainably manage their farms, such as by using shade crops that will keep the watershed intact and protect water quality downstream for urban residents. USAID/Dominican Republic is developing similar schemes for Santo Domingo and other areas in the Dominican Republic.

In communities along rivers and the coast, storm surges and floods are often exacerbated because of degradation of mangroves, coral reefs, and wetlands. These natural resources not only are critical for tourism and fishing-dependent livelihoods, but also provide natural protection against climate impacts, such as strong storms and waves. In Samaná, USAID/Dominican Republic is working with fishing cooperatives to improve management of fishing operations and to protect mangroves, reefs, and fish populations. In Santo Domingo, USAID's Office of Disaster Assistance has supported the Dominican Institute for Integrated Development to reduce the risk of flooding in poor neighborhoods by keeping storm drainage systems unclogged through improved waste management and improving natural drainage through reforestation projects.

USAID/Dominican Republic is also increasing the access of vulnerable populations to financial and risk management tools, enabling them to independently take adaptive actions, such as installing portable water towers on a small farm or expanding urban green spaces to capture rainwater and reduce flooding. In rural areas, small farmers will also soon benefit from a USAID-funded climate index insurance product that will protect them from certain climate risks, such as drought and strong storms, and improve their likelihood of successfully accessing other important financial tools, such as credit. By 2018 USAID/Dominican Republic will protect water resources, reduce disaster risks, and help small farmers and other vulnerable populations access tools to help them adapt to global climate change.

Sub-IR 2.2.1: Individual and Institutional Knowledge of Adaptation Strategies Increased
Indicator:
- Number of adaptation strategies tested and adopted

USAID/Dominican Republic will support implementation of actions to protect people and property at the watershed, coastal and local levels. For example, at the watershed level, by engaging irrigation user groups in the lower Yaque watershed to improve their irrigation efficiency and decrease their output of chemical wastes, the water supply and coral reefs in the coastal town of Monte Cristi can be protected. At the local level, in marginal neighborhoods, community groups could be organized into water and sanitation committees to work with the municipal water utilities to conserve water, protect existing water infrastructure, and jointly program new investments. In coastal areas, municipal governments, civil society, environmental organizations, and the private sector, such as tourism operators, could be linked to each other and to the Ministries of Tourism and Environment to promote reef and mangrove restoration.

Sub-IR 2.2.2: Increased Access of Vulnerable Populations to Technical and Financial Tools
Indicator:
- Number of climate mitigation and/or adaptation tools, technologies and methodologies developed, tested and/or adopted

In order to scale up the implementation of adaptive measures, vulnerable populations must have access to technical and financial tools to implement measures on their own. Utilizing the lessons learned from testing strategies under Sub-IR 2.2.1, USAID/Dominican Republic will provide technical tools and assistance on effective adaptation strategies. For example, in communities with unstable drinking water supply, support could be given for community water management. In communities with persistent flooding and landslides, assistance could be given on maintaining stabilizing vegetation, improving drainage, and improving waste management systems within their communities. This assistance will be channeled through coalitions and partnerships with actors like FEDOMU, the Ministry of Environment, the National Climate Change Council, universities, and NGOs, who have communication networks that reach many people to deliver information and training. The strategy will also leverage existing networks, such as youth groups and Climaccion, which is an online platform connecting organizations working on climate change.

USAID/Dominican Republic will also help vulnerable populations access financing that is already offered by banks, micro finance institutions, insurance companies, and governments. For example, USAID/Dominican Republic will also support expansion of water funds and payment for ecological services to protect critical watersheds and water resources for growing urban areas.

By the end of this strategy, priority drinking water sources for both Santo Domingo and Santiago will be protected by improved upper watershed management. Groundwater sources will be protected through improved groundwater extraction management. Targeted coastal communities will better protect their coastal infrastructure, such as fisheries, coral reefs, mangroves, and beach habitats. Lastly, marginal communities in urban areas will have reduced their risk from climate-related disasters, such as flooding and landslides.

Policy Dialogue

While concentrating efforts at the local level, USAID/Dominican Republic will pursue dialogue with national government entities, such as the Ministry of Economy, Planning, and Development (MEPyD), the Ministries of Tourism and Environment, and the National Climate Change Council to harmonize land use, development, and natural resource planning at all levels, as well as increase involvement of municipal governments in national level decision-making processes. USAID/Dominican Republic will also engage the government at the national and municipal levels to support participatory, transparent budget processes.

Partnerships

USAID/Dominican Republic assistance will continue developing holistic approaches to climate change adaptation by leveraging the work of other partners, such as the German Society for International Cooperation's work in forestry and the World Bank and European Union's work in municipal governance, for knowledge-sharing, capacity building, and technical assistance in the Dominican Republic.

1. GODR

USAID/Dominican Republic will support the GODR's 2030 National Development Plan's objective of improving the climate resilience of the Dominican people. This DO will support the specific objective of designing and implementing land use plans that facilitate the integrated management of risk, regulate land use, and encourage the sustainable use of natural resources.[57] This strategy also supports

---

[57] Dominican Republic National Development Strategy (2010-2030)

the country's National Adaptation Plan of Action and its priorities of water source protection, agriculture, and protection of coastal/marine resources.[58]

The Mission's program will also support the GODR's decentralization objective. USAID/Dominican Republic will specifically connect municipalities with broader planning processes, such as with MEPyD and the Ministry of Environment on the National Land Use Plan and the Ministry of Tourism on the National Tourism Plan. In order to ensure project sustainability, connections will also be made with the Ministry of Environment, water utilities, tourism clusters (which have been supported by USAID/Dominican Republic), universities, and FEDOMU. Additionally, USAID/Dominican Republic will leverage the engagement of the National Council on Climate Change in a UN-funded climate change education program that increases the flow of climate information to a wide variety of audiences, from youth to journalists.

2. Donors

USAID/Dominican Republic will build on the success of other donors, such as the World Bank, in strengthening the technical and financial capacity of thirty municipalities through its $20 million Municipal Development Project.[59] The IDB is also contributing to local capacity development in Santo Domingo via $1 million in assistance to planning units. At the national level, USAID/Dominican Republic will build on work already conducted by the World Bank and the IDB to develop national-level insurance schemes to compensate for climate change-related losses. Support is also already being provided by the European Union and UNDP to the Dominican Climate Change Council. The Food and Agriculture Organization is providing assistance in the area of Food Security and Climate Change. The Government of Spain is working on global climate change and natural resource management issues in Enriquillo and the German Government has two GCC activities that complement USAID/Dominican Republic's work in ecosystem-based adaptation and micro insurance.

3. Private Sector and Civil Society

The private sector has become more active in the arena of climate change adaptation, particularly through the tourism clusters that USAID/Dominican Republic currently supports. This strategy will support the creation of additional coalitions to work jointly on environmental issues, such as coastal protection and beach restoration. Civil society organizations, such as environmental NGOs, are increasingly leading the country with respect to climate change and, given their strength, USAID/Dominican Republic envisions partnering with local organizations to implement many of these GCC activities.

---

[58] Dominican Republic National Adaptation Plan of Action
[59] http://www.worldbank.org/en/country/dominicanrepublic

Development Objective 3: AIDS-free Generation Advanced

Indicators:

- Percentage of infants born to HIV-infected mothers who are positive for HIV
- HIV prevalence among key populations

On November 8, 2011, former Secretary of State Clinton laid out a vision of an AIDS-free generation; one where "virtually no children are born with the virus. As these children become teenagers and adults, they are at far lower risk of becoming infected than they would be today thanks to a wide range of prevention tools, and if they do acquire HIV, they have access to treatment that helps prevent them from developing AIDS and passing the virus on to others." USAID/Dominican Republic's third Development Objective will advance this vision in the Dominican Republic.

Achieving this Development Objective will contribute to the overall CDCS goal of improving citizen security to promote economic growth because "nations with healthy populations are more likely to be productive, prosperous, and peaceful…Conversely, … Nations with high numbers of unhealthy citizens are more likely to be poor, badly governed, weak, and prone to instability or even conflict."[60] The economic impact of HIV/AIDS also has both direct and indirect impacts on a nation's economic prospects.[61] The direct costs associated with HIV include treatment associated with HIV-related illness, which has serious implications for health care budgets and higher medical costs for HIV victims. Indirect costs are associated with the losses to the economy, and to the victims and their families, including the loss of value of production, the loss of current wages, the cost of absenteeism, higher recruitment costs, and the loss of household savings for victims and their families.

In addition to preventing these losses to individuals, families and the economy as a whole, by reducing HIV/AIDS and the stigma and discrimination related to the disease, USAID/Dominican Republic will also build social justice, promote and protect human rights, and enhance the security of vulnerable populations in accordance with the Inter-American Democratic Charter.[62] In doing so, the economy will benefit from a more inclusive and healthy society, and democratic stability will be strengthened by promoting inclusiveness and building social equity. Building social equity requires participation by a wide range of stakeholders, including central government, civil society, businesses, media, and academia, and strong representation from women and young people, all of whom contribute to providing the basic social services, skills, and opportunities that allow vulnerable populations to participate fully in society. In the Dominican Republic, key HIV populations include populations with HIV (PwHIV), men who have sex with men, sex workers, residents of bateyes and drug users. In addition, marginalized groups, such as residents of bateyes and poor urban neighborhoods, women and girls, persons with disabilities, and Haitians or Dominicans of Haitian descent are subject to exclusion, stigma, discrimination, and violence.[63] USAID/DR funding will be designed to increase inclusion, and improve access, prevention, and treatment.

---

[60] Admiral William J. Fallon, CSIS: Global Health as a Bridge to Security, p. v, http://csis.org/files/publication/120920_Downie_GlobalHealthSecurity_Web.pdf

[61] Balyamujura, H., Jooste, A., van Schalkwyk, H., and Carstens, J. (2000) Impact of the HIV/AIDS pandemic on the demand for food in South Africa

[69]Inter-American Democratic Charter, Lima, 2001, http://www.oas.org/charter/docs/resolution1_en_p4.htm

[63] HPP Health Policy Project. 2012. Stigma and Discrimination and Gender-Based Violence Participatory Assessment. Futures Group International.

Intermediate Result 3.1: Quality of HIV Response Improved
Indicators:
- Percentage of key populations reporting the use of a condom at last high risk sex act
- Number of HIV-positive pregnant women who received antiretrovirals (ARVs) to reduce risk of mother-to-child-transmission

In order for the Dominican Republic to advance an AIDS-free generation, USAID/Dominican Republic will concentrate its resources on improving the quality of the HIV response. USAID/Dominican Republic is only able to focus in this concentrated way because of the other resources available through Dominican and development partners for inputs, such as infrastructure, human resources, and medicines (described below). Ninety-five percent of pregnant women complete four antenatal care visits, and 98 percent of births are attended by a skilled birth attendant.[64] With other program elements already addressed, USAID/Dominican Republic can now focus all its attention on improving the quality of care.

The Dominican National Health Plan identifies *quality* as the principal challenge of the health sector.[65] Poor quality is linked to limitations in clinical and administrative management, limited staff supervision and other institutional weaknesses in the health sector.[66] In HIV services, symptomatic of poor quality in the health sector are the high rates of stigma and discrimination suffered by persons with HIV and key populations at both public and private facilities, which in turn limits their access to quality care and services, particularly from the public sector.[67] The 2008 Stigma Index showed that nearly a quarter of persons with HIV reported having their human rights violated, while ten percent reported having been refused a job as a result of their HIV status. The 2007 DHS found that only 15.2 percent of men and 23.5 percent of women expressed accepting attitudes toward people living with HIV.

Evidence from other parts of the health sector has radically changed the belief among hospital and Ministry of Health staff that quality is a long and complex process. Rather, there is now a better understanding that quality can be improved by using readily available tools and taking hospital teams through systematic self-assessments, devising solutions within their capabilities, and setting realistic goals and deadlines.[68] As such, USAID/Dominican Republic will focus on improving the quality of the HIV response to strengthen the capacity of the Dominican Republic to advance towards an AIDS-free generation.

In the Dominican context, and building on USAID/Dominican Republic's comparative advantage from previous work in HIV prevention and treatment, USAID/Dominican Republic has identified three areas to improve the quality of HIV services: (1) HIV prevention for key populations strengthened, including HIV testing and counseling, condoms and other evidence-based prevention activities; (2) Access to services increased for PwHIV, including Prevention of Mother to Child Transmission (PMTCT) and Positive Health, Dignity, and Prevention (PHDP); and (3) Health system strengthened.

---

[64] 2007 Demographic and Health Survey
[65] Dominican Republic National Health Plan 2006-2015. Ministry of Health.
[66] Rathe. M. & Moliné, A. (2011) The Health System of the Dominican Republic. Salud Publica Mexico, 53:2.
[67] Kerrigan, D. & Barrington, C. (2012) Exploring the positive health, dignity and prevention needs of female sex workers, men who have sex with men and transgender women in the Dominican Republic and Swaziland.
[68] USAID Maternal and Child Health Performance Evaluation. 2012. Global Health Tech.

Sub-IR 3.1.1: HIV Prevention for Key Populations Strengthened
Indicator:

- Number of key populations reached with individual and/or small group level HIV preventive interventions

"To achieve an AIDS-free generation, countries must target efforts where the virus is—reaching and supporting those populations at greatest risk and urgently needing services."[69] Statistics from the 2007 DHS survey show that those with the greatest need are female sex workers, men who have sex with men, transgender individuals, drug users, and residents of *bateyes*. In order to strengthen HIV prevention for these key populations, USAID/Dominican Republic will work with a network of CSOs to expand the reach of prevention interventions and make them more effective by ensuring the minimum package of services are offered to key populations, including access to condoms; HIV testing; HIV care and treatment; and STI screening and treatment.[70] Activities will also address underlying risk factors such as transactional and intergenerational sex and poor condom use among regular partners of female sex workers.

"Stigma, discrimination and fear of violence or legal sanctions often undermine access of key populations to health care, including HIV services."[71] USAID/Dominican Republic will work with CSOs and the GODR to identify barriers to services; develop and implement plans of action to overcome these barriers; and monitor implementation.

Sub-IR 3.1.2: Services for People with HIV Improved
Indicators:

- Number of pregnant women with known HIV status
- Number of People Living with HIV/AIDS (PLHIV) reached with Positive Health Dignity and Prevention interventions

"Preventing new HIV infections among children and keeping their mothers alive is not only a moral imperative, it is also one of the best investments the world can make to address AIDS. Through comprehensive PMTCT programs, we not only keep mothers and babies alive and healthy, we also support healthier and more productive families and communities."[72] As part of the *Regional Initiative for the Elimination of Mother-to-Child Transmission of HIV and Congenital Syphilis in Latin America and the Caribbean*, the Dominican Republic has committed to reducing the rate of mother-to-child transmission of HIV.

A critical challenge for the PMTCT program is the number of women, not identified until labor and delivery, who are HIV infected. This reduces the effectiveness of a PMTCT program. In 2011, 81 percent of women diagnosed nationwide with HIV received ARVs to prevent vertical transmission.[73]

---

[69] PEPFAR Blueprint, page 5, www.pepfar.gov/documents/organization/201386.pdf
[70] Key Population TDY Report, Key Populations Working Group, December, 2012
[71] PEPFAR Blueprint, page 29, www.pepfar.gov/documents/organization/201386.pdf
[72] PEPFAR Blueprint, www.pepfar.gov/documents/organization/201386.pdf
[73] National Report on the Progress Achieved in the Country: Follow-up on the Declaration of Commitment to HIV/AIDS. March 2012.
www.unaids.org/en/dataanalysis/knowyourresponse/countryprogressreports/2012countries/ce_DO_Narrative_Report[1].pdf

At USAID/Dominican Republic supported hospitals, rapid HIV tests have resulted in 92 percent of women tested receiving same day results and 86 percent of women diagnosed with HIV receiving ARVs. The Dominican Republic has significantly improved antiretroviral treatment coverage among eligible patients from 63 percent in 2010 to 89 percent in 2011, but only 82 percent continued with ART for more than a year,[74] indicating significant issues with adherence to medicine regimes and the quality of patient care. As a result, in USAID-supported public facilities, the MTCT rate was 2.6 percent in 2012.[75]

To expand the PMTCT program nationwide, the government has launched its own National Elimination of Mother to Child Transmission (eMTCT) Strategy, which prioritizes 16 hospitals based on birth volume and HIV prevalence. In order to meet our goal to reduce and sustain a MTCT rate below 2 percent by 2018, USAID/Dominican Republic will invest its resources in the following activities: Align with the National eMTCT Strategy by expanding technical assistance to the 16 priority hospitals; provide technical assistance at the central and service delivery levels; build the capacity of the GODR to provide supportive site supervision; and strengthen the supply chain of medicines and supplies in the public health sector, including antiretrovirals.[76]

"Implementation of comprehensive positive health, dignity, and prevention interventions for PLHIV is also an important HIV prevention approach."[77] PHDP programs aim to reduce morbidity and mortality, reduce HIV incidence, and reduce HIV-related stigma and discrimination for persons living with HIV.[78] In FY 2012, USAID/Dominican Republic reached more than 9,000 PwHIV with PHDP, representing more than 20 percent of the estimated number of PwHIV.[79] USAID/Dominican Republic is currently supporting operations research to test effective models of PHDP with key populations.[80] Findings from these studies will inform future programming of PHDP, which will allow for an expanded reach and a more comprehensive biomedical and behavioral package for PwHIV.

Sub-IR 3.1.3: Health System Strengthened
Indicators:
- Percentage of total GODR funding for HIV NGOs
- Number of healthcare workers who successfully completed an in-service training program
- Percentage of health care facilities that have available a shortlist of essential HIV and TB medicines

---

[74] http://www.unaids.org/en/dataanalysis/knowyourresponse/countryprogressreports/2012countries/ce_DO_Narrative_Report[1].pdf

[75] FHI360. Strengthening HIV Services in Regions V and VII Final Project Report, 2013.

[76] PMTCT Technical Working Group

[77] PEPFAR Blueprint PEPFAR Blueprint, www.pepfar.gov/documents/organization/201386.pdf

[78] Exploring the Positive Health, Dignity and Prevention Needs of Female Sex Workers, Men Who Have Sex with Men and Transgender Women in the Dominican Republic and Swaziland, March 2013 http://www.jhsph.edu/research/centers-and-institutes/research-to-prevention/publications/PHDP-19March2013-final.pdf

[79] FY 2012 PEPFAR Annual Progress Report for the Dominican Republic.

[80] Exploring the Positive Health, Dignity and Prevention Needs of Female Sex Workers, Men Who Have Sex with Men and Transgender Women in the Dominican Republic and Swaziland, March 2013 http://www.jhsph.edu/research/centers-and-institutes/research-to-prevention/publications/PHDP-19March2013-final.pdf

USAID/Dominican Republic will focus its health systems investment in four areas: (1) stewardship, accountability, and management; (2) human resources for health; (3) supply chain management; and (4) strategic information.

Stewardship, Accountability, and Management

Country ownership is "the end state where a nation's efforts are led, implemented, and eventually paid for by its government, communities, civil society and private sector … it is principally about building the capacity to set priorities, manage resources, develop plans, and carry them out."[81] USAID is committed to country ownership and will continue to invest in the capacity of local institutions, including the GODR and CSOs, to ensure the sustainability of the national HIV response.

The 2012 USAID/Dominican Republic Maternal and Child Health evaluation highlighted investments in improving the management capacity of public hospitals and the different levels of the Ministry of Health as "success facilitators" and clearly identified the need to continue investing in management capacity.[82] Under this strategy, USAID/Dominican Republic will work with the GODR to increase engagement with civil society organizations working in health, considering the pivotal role and contributions of CSOs to the national HIV Response - CSOs provide approximately 25 percent of HIV treatment services[83] and nearly all community prevention and care services for key populations and people living with HIV.

USAID/Dominican Republic has already invested significant resources in expanding the management capacity of local CSOs. These groups are often dependent on support from international organizations and donors rather than local entities like the GODR or the private sector. It is critical that their management capacity is strengthened and that they find innovative ways to generate revenue in order to achieve sustainability.

USAID/Dominican Republic will also leverage resources to support the development and implementation of a National NGO Sustainability Strategy. This will include mapping the location and capacity of all CSOs working on the HIV response, developing their capacity through training, and helping them to become financially sustainable. USAID/Dominican Republic will also continue to strengthen the capacity of both the public sector and CSOs assistance and continue to provide direct financial support to CSOs as they transition to more sustainable funding.

With regard to capacity-building, "PEPFAR (HIV/AIDS) programs will prioritize capacity-building and systems-strengthening interventions that build strong leadership and governance, particularly those that strengthen the social service workforce and system."[84]

Under this strategy, USAID/Dominican Republic will continue to support the GODR to improve human resource management in the health sector; establish a human resources information system, and train a cadre of human resource specialists for the health sector. USAID/Dominican Republic will also

---

[81] Secretary Clinton, June 2012, secondary from PEPFAR Blueprint
[82] USAID Maternal and Child Health Mid-Term Performance Evaluation. 2012. GH Tech
[83] Dirección General de Control de las Infecciones de Transmisión Sexual y SIDA (DIGECITSS)
[84] PEPFAR Blueprint, www.pepfar.gov/documents/organization/201386.pdf

help the GODR to establish a more efficient human resources system to improve the capacity of the health system to provide quality health and HIV services.

Supply Chain Management

A 2011 USAID-supported assessment showed that the GODR paid two to three times the international market price for medicines.[85] In addition, the highly centralized supply chain management system contributed to local stock outs of ARVs, test kits, and laboratory reagents. In response to these inefficiencies, USAID/Dominican Republic supported the MOH to implement a National Pharmaceutical Management System, which simultaneously centralizes procurement while de-centralizing distribution in order to maximize efficiencies.

Currently, USAID/Dominican Republic is supporting the consolidation of all of the GODR's medical procurements under the GODR's Public Procurement Agent of Medicines. As a result of this reform, the GODR has the potential to reduce the procurement cost of medicines by up to 60 percent.

In addition to the support currently being provided, under this strategy USAID/Dominican Republic will strengthen pharmaceutical management systems at service delivery sites, improve the rational use of pharmaceuticals, reduce the number of treatment regimens, introduce fixed-dose combinations, and identify financing alternatives to the Global Fund to ensure a sustainable supply of ARVs. To further promote transparency and accountability, USAID/Dominican Republic will help the GODR to develop an annual catalog of medicines and supplies, which includes price lists and preferred vendors for medicines, which cannot be procured centrally. This will increase efficiencies and transparency.

Strategic Information

Improved planning and decision-making for the healthcare system requires better collection, analysis, and use of data. A 2006 USG assessment of surveillance for sexually transmitted infections and HIV/AIDS in the Dominican Republic highlighted the lack of a unified reporting system, over-centralization, lack of computer infrastructure, significant delays in data transmission, absence of case reporting by smaller public health centers, and few surveillance training opportunities for staff.[86]

Therefore, the USG and other donors are supporting the implementation of several surveys. Within eighteen months, the country will have data from the 2012 Behavioral Surveillance Survey (BSS) for Sex Workers, MSM, and Drug Users, the 2013 Demographic and Health Survey, the 2013 BSS for Haitians and Haitian-Dominicans, and the 2013 Antenatal (ANC) Sentinel Surveillance Survey.

Meanwhile, the Hospital Management Information System (SIGHO), being implemented under the USAID/Dominican Republic Maternal and Child Health Centers of Excellence Project, has performed well in the ten hospitals where it has been implemented.[87] SIGHO allows, for the first time, for these facilities to have an information system that links information from the patient registry, patient records,

---

[85] SPS Strengthening Pharmaceutical Systems. 2011. Supply Chain Assessment. Management Sciences for Health.
[86] Characterization of the Epidemiological Surveillance System of the DR, CDC/GAP, 2006.
[87]USAID/DR: Evaluation of USAID's MCH Performance, Intermediate Result 4, May 2012;
https//dec.usaid.gov/dec/blog/postreview

and the pharmacy, which facilitates instant access to all relevant information about a patient and prevents duplicative and lost patient records.

Under this strategy, USAID/Dominican Republic will support the implementation and use of systematic and cost-effective data collection systems and studies, such as the MOH's new HIV Patient Monitoring Record, and the expansion of SIGHO. With CSOs, local organizations will be able to better target and measure interventions. Decision-making in the health system must be guided by sound information; therefore improving the collection, analysis and use of information for decision-making is critical to improving the quality of health services.

Policy Dialogue

The Mission has identified five policy priorities as a result of this strategy development process: (1) the Mission will engage the GODR and the private sector to mobilize resources to ensure the sustainability of CSOs and HIV services for key populations; (2) the Mission will work with the Ministry of Health, the National HIV/AIDS Council, and health insurance entities to ensure the financing of ARVs as the Global Fund draws down; (3) the Mission will continue to promote transparency through the reform of public procurement of medicines and supplies and civil service reform; (4) the Mission will work with the Ministry of Health to institutionalize and expand the Maternal Child Health Centers of Excellence Model nationwide; and (5) the Mission will work with the GODR to better address critical issues like stigma and discrimination and gender-based violence, especially among vulnerable populations.

Partnerships

1. GODR

The CDCS is aligned with and supports the Dominican Republic National Health Plan 2006-2015 and the Dominican Republic National Strategic Plan to Prevent and Control STIs and HIV/AIDS 2007-2015. As described in these documents, the government serves three functions as part of the National HIV response: (1) the MOH's General Directorate for the Control of STIs and AIDS provides stewardship over the health system's response to HIV; (2) the Directorate of Development and Strengthening of the Regional Health Service Networks provides health services; and (3) the National HIV/AIDS Council provides oversight of the National HIV Response.

Improving healthcare quality also continues to be a policy priority for the GODR. In 2008, the MOH established a Vice Minister in charge of Quality Assurance. In 2011, the MOH launched the formulation of the National Quality Assurance Policy. The Minister of Health announced he plans to expand this program nationwide. In 2014, USAID/Dominican Republic will be transferring responsibility for the Centers of Excellence program to the MOH. In 2013, the formal adoption of the Centers of Excellence certification process by the Ministry of Health helps guarantee the expansion of this model nationwide.

As illustrated in the 2008 National AIDS Spending Assessment, the GODR's tax generated revenues devoted specifically to the National HIV Response were 16.1 percent of the total, as compared to 48.7 percent coming from international donors and 24.7 percent coming from out-of-pocket expenses. As part of the latest agreement with the Global Fund, the GODR will assume progressively more responsibility for the cost of ARVs. In 2013, the GODR is responsible for 30 percent of the costs of

ARVs; in 2014, 60 percent; and in 2015, 90 percent. In response to its increased financial responsibility for funding HIV programs, for the first time, in 2013 the GODR assigned $1.9 million for the procurement of ARVs.

2. Donors

The Global Fund Country Coordination Mechanism, in which USAID/Dominican Republic and other USG PEPFAR agencies are active participants, is an important forum for donor coordination. The current Global Fund agreement for HIV/AIDS totals $87 million and is scheduled to end in 2015. The principal recipients of the Global Fund provide limited funding to CSOs to provide HIV prevention and home-based care services for PwHIV, procure ARVs, test kits, lab reagents, and other commodities, and pay for healthcare personnel. Unfortunately, under the *New Funding Model* of the Global Fund, it will be increasingly difficult for upper-middle income countries like the Dominican Republic to access these resources in the future.

The other international organizations providing support in the area of HIV are: the Pan American Health Organization/World Health Organization (PAHO/WHO), United Nations Children's Fund (UNICEF), and the Joint United Nations Programme on HIV/AIDS. PAHO/WHO and UNICEF are providing technical assistance to the GODR for Elimination of Mother to Child Transmission, to support prevention of mother-to-child transmission.

The World Bank and the Inter-American Development Bank support health sector reform more broadly, mostly through infrastructure investments. The European Union provides budget support to move forward civil service reform, including the Health Career Law. USAID/Dominican Republic has conducted assessments and produced designs for nine regional medical warehouses that are needed for the National Pharmaceutical Management System to become fully operational. The GODR complemented these efforts by mobilizing resources from other donors to finance the specific recommended improvements.

3. **Private Sector and Civil Society**

The National Health Plan and National Strategic Plan also describe the important contributions of the private sector and civil society in terms of service provision and oversight. CSOs are especially important partners due to their critical role as HIV prevention, care, and treatment service providers for key populations. USAID/Dominican Republic will continue to provide resources to these organizations (including more direct funding) and technical assistance to improve the quality of services provided by CSOs; and to advocate for the sustainability of the National HIV Response. Finally, the private sector is becoming more engaged through corporate social responsibility programs. USAID/Dominican Republic will increase its engagement with the private sector to mobilize resources, including in areas where USAID/Dominican Republic support has ended, such as Maternal and Child Health.

Building local evaluation capacity

Strong performance monitoring and evaluation are essential for ensuring effective management and results achievement in USAID's support to the DR National Health Plan. USAID/Dominican Republic will seek opportunities to engage directly with the government and Nongovernmental Organizations (NGOs) to address issues related to deficiencies or lack of monitoring and evaluation (M&E) capacity.

The successful implementation of USAID Forward procurement reform goals requires local institutions to develop not just the capacity to manage and administer funds, but also the capacity to monitor and evaluate projects. Developing the monitoring and evaluation capacity of the GODR will empower host country officials to effectively manage their programs, account for resources and deliver evidence to inform policy-making. In addition, M&E capacity and good information systems will also help civil society organizations to more effectively advocate for accountability and transparency in the allocation and expenditure of pubic budgets.

In the past year, USAID/Dominican Republic has identified several Dominican analysts and Dominican private sector think tanks that have produced thoughtful studies of Dominican development problems. USAID/Dominican Republic will initiate a more systematic assessment of local partners, including Dominican universities, technical colleges, think tanks, CSOs, and private sector research firms and, in support of USAID Forward objectives, seek to contract much more with local partners than in the past.

Annex 1: Results Framework

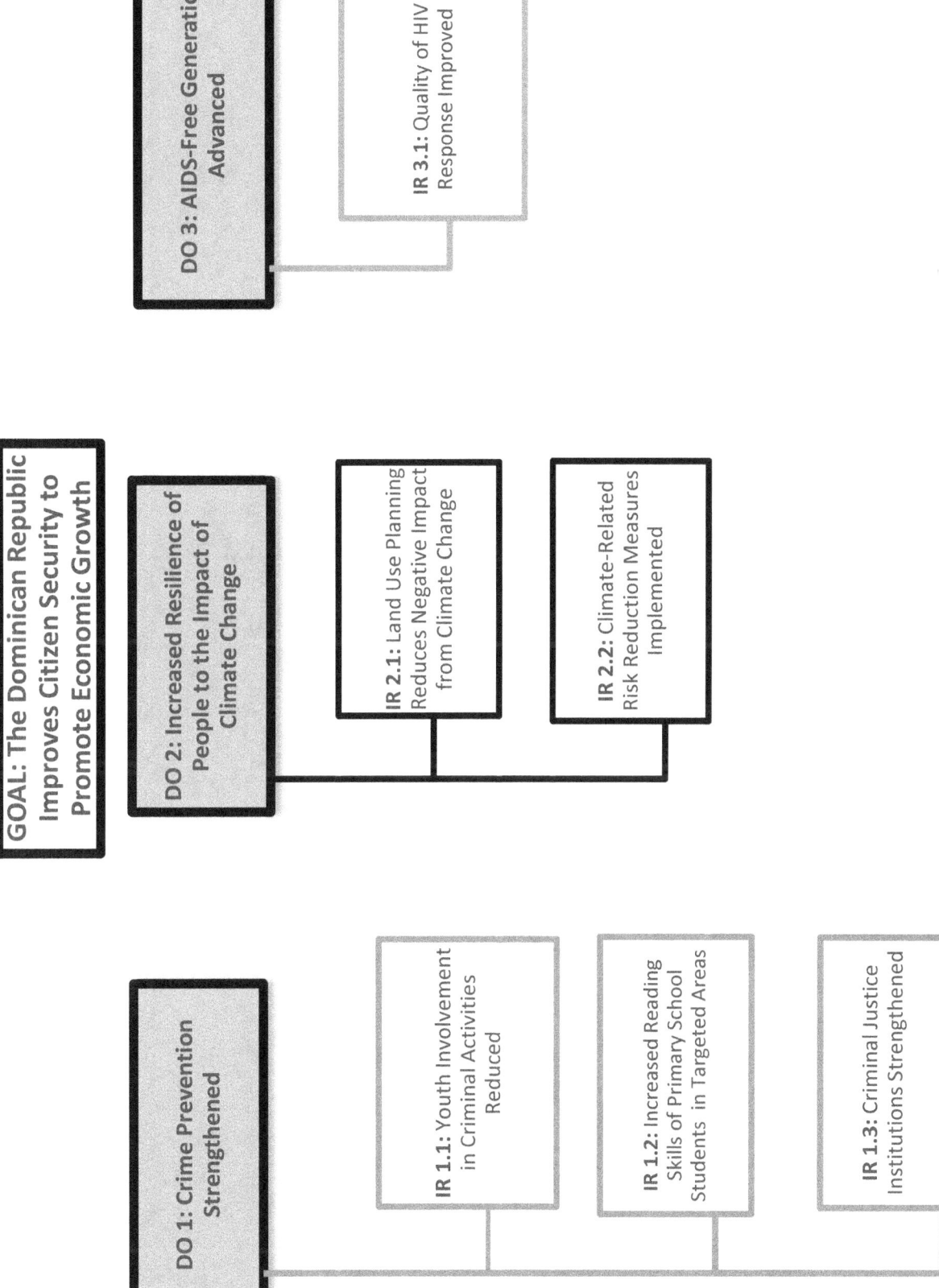

Annexes

GOAL: The Dominican Republic Improves Citizen Security to Promote Economic Growth

DO 1: Crime Prevention Strengthened

IR 1.1: Youth Involvement in Criminal Activities Reduced

IR 1.2: Increased Reading Skills of Primary School Students in Targeted Areas

IR 1.3: Criminal Justice Institutions Strengthened

DO 2: Increased Resilience of People to the Impact of Climate Change

IR 2.1: Land Use Planning Reduces Negative Impact from Climate Change

IR 2.2: Climate-Related Risk Reduction Measures Implemented

DO 3: AIDS-Free Generation Advanced

IR 3.1: Quality of HIV Response Improved

Annex 2: Acronyms and Abbreviations

ADR	Alternative Dispute Resolution
AIDS	Acquired Immune Deficiency Syndrome
ARCC	African and Latin American Resilience to Climate Change
ARV	Antiretroviral
BSS	Behavioral Surveillance Survey
CBSI	Caribbean Basin Security Initiative
CCT	Conditional Cash Transfer
CDCS	Country Development Cooperation Strategy
CSO	Civil Society Organization
DHS	Demographic and Health Survey
DNP	Dominican National Police
DO	Development Objective
DR	Dominican Republic
DU	Drug User
EGRA	Early Grade Reading Assessment
eMTCT	Elimination of Mother to Child Transmission
ESP	Effective Schools Program
FEDOMU	Federation of Municipalities
FY	Fiscal Year
GBV	Gender-Based Violence
GCC	Global Climate Change
GDP	Gross Domestic Product
GODR	Government of the Dominican Republic
HIV	Human Immunodeficiency Virus
IDB	Inter-American Development Bank
IDEC	Dominican Initiative for Quality Education
INDHRI	National Institute for Hydrological Resources
LAPOP	Latin American Public Opinion Project
LGBT	Lesbian, Gay, Bisexual, and Transgender
M&E	Monitoring and Evaluation
MEPyD	Ministry of Economy, Planning and Development
MOE	Ministry of Education
MOH	Ministry of Health
MSM	Men Who Have Sex With Men
MTCT	Mother to Child Transmission
NGO	Nongovernmental Organization
ONAMET	National Meteorology Office

PAHO/WHO	Pan American Health Organization/World Health Organization
PEPFAR	U.S. President's Emergency Plan for AIDS Relief
PHDP	Positive Health, Dignity, and Prevention
PLHIV	Persons Living with HIV
PMTCT	Prevention of Mother to Child Transmission
PwHIV	Persons With HIV
SERCE	Second Regional Comparative and Explanatory Study
SIGHO	Hospital Management Information System
TB	Tuberculosis
UNDP	United Nations Development Programme
UNESCO	United Nations Educational, Scientific, and Cultural Organization
UNFPA	United Nations Population Fund
UNICEF	United Nations Children's Fund
USG	United States Government
WB	World Bank
WEF	World Economic Forum
WHO	World Health Organization

1. Analyses completed

As the CDCS must be grounded in evidence and analysis, the Mission has completed, updated or reviewed the following USAID/USG analyses to inform its strategy design:

- 2013 Gender Analysis
- 2011 Tropical Rainforest and Bio-diversity Analysis
- 2013 Democracy, Human Rights, and Governance Assessment
- 2013 Global Climate Change Vulnerability Assessment
- 2009 Gender Assessment
- 2010 Youth Assessment
- 2011 Economic Growth program evaluation
- 2011 Trafficking in Persons assessment
- 2012 Dominican Republic Global Health Initiative Strategy
- 2012 Human Rights Report
- 2013 Mid-term Evaluation of the Education Portfolio
- PEPFAR Program Review
- 2007 Demographic Health Survey
- 2010 and 2012 Americas Barometer surveys
- 2013 USAID/Dominican Republic Disabilities Inclusion Action Plan
- 2012 Information Communications and Technology Assessment
- 2013 Dominican Republic Property Rights and Land Tenure Profile
- 2012 USAID Maternal and Child Health Portfolio Evaluation

2. Other Analyses

Additionally, the Mission drew upon evidence from multiple assessments, evaluations, and other analyses completed by the Government of the Dominican Republic, civil society, the private sector, foundations, regional organizations, international organizations, and other donors. Chief among them are:

- Dominican Republic National Development Strategy 2010-2030 (GODR)
- Caribbean Human Development Report 2012: Human Development and the Shift to Better Citizen Security (UNDP)
- "Constructing a Better Future for the Dominican Republic" by International Development Center of Harvard University
- World Bank Cost of Doing Business Report
- World Bank CAS 2009-2013
- UNDP Latin America and Caribbean Regional Human Development Report 2010
- Transparency International Report, December 2012
- CEPAL Report, December 2012
- World Bank and WHO Report on Persons with Disabilities, 2011
- 2011 World Development Report Conflict, Security and Development Report
- Crime, Violence and Development: Trends, Costs, and Policy Options in the Caribbean, UNDP, 2007

- Does Crime Lower Growth? Evidence from Colombia, Working Paper, Commission on Growth and Development
- Perceived Returns to Education and the Demand for Schooling, Robert Jensen, Quarterly Journal of Economics, May 2010

USAID/Dominican Republic completed 40 meetings and consultations with the following entities over the course of the strategy development period.

1. Office of the Vice President
2. Ministry of Economy, Planning and Development
3. Ministry of the Presidency
4. Ministry of Education
5. Ministry of Health
6. Ministry of Youth
7. Ministry of Environment
8. Ministry of Agriculture
9. Ministry of Finance
10. Attorney General
11. LGBT organizations
12. GBV organizations
13. Persons with Disabilities organizations
14. Mayor of Santiago
15. Mayor of San Pedro de Macoris
16. Private sector
17. Implementing partners
18. Donors at World Bank
19. UNDP
20. UNICEF
21. UNOPS
22. UNFPA
23. European Commission
24. IDB
25. GIZ
26. Consul of Belgium
27. USG Agencies at Post